A SELECTED ANNOTATED BIBLIOGRAPHY
ON ITALIAN SERIAL COMPOSERS

A SELECTED ANNOTATED BIBLIOGRAPHY
ON ITALIAN SERIAL COMPOSERS

Harvey J. Stokes

Studies in the History and Interpretation of Music
Volume 27

THE EDWIN MELLEN PRESS
Lewiston/Queenston/Lampeter

Library of Congress Cataloging-in-Publication Data

This book has been registered with the Library of Congress.

This is volume 27 in the continuing series
Studies in The History and Interpretation of Music
Volume 27 ISBN 0-88946-577-0
SHIM series ISBN 0-88946-426-X

A CIP catalog record for this book
is available from the British Library.

The Edwin Mellen Press
Box 450
Lewiston, New York
USA 14092

The Edwin Mellen Press
Box 67
Queenston, Ontario
CANADA L0S 1L0

The Edwin Mellen Press, Ltd.
Lampeter, Dyfed, Wales
UNITED KINGDOM SA48 7DY

Printed in the United States of America

to Charlotte
and the
kids

TABLE OF CONTENTS

PREFACE

John Vinton's *Dictionary of 20th-Century Music* contains an article which discusses the musical trends of modern-day Italy. Within this article, there are succinct but informative comments on prominent dodecaphonic[1] composers. Eleven of the composers discussed in that article receive attention in this present work; much general reference is made also about the Italian avant-garde composition scene.

Contained herewith through library research are listings of important articles and books on the aforementioned areas. These documents take the form of interviews, musical critiques and analyses, stylistic surveys, biographies, and listings of compositions.[2] Helpful sources used for these lists include *The Music Index*, *Dissertation Abstracts*, *Jahrbuch der Musikbibliothek Peters* and *Serial Music* (by Ann Basart).

After committing the bibliographical information to over 600 3x5 cards, screening to determine book or article relevancy[3] was performed; thus 478 cards

---

[1]A discussion of trends in Italian dodecaphonic and avant-garde music is presented in Vinton's Dictionary of 20th-Century Music. This seems to be useful in as much as the body of creative work by the composers mentioned in the article represents not just dodecaphony (classical serialism), but a wide range of compositional possibilities also (such as, for example, multi-media, chance/alea, non-serial neo-classicism, and electronic music). Nevertheless, these composers will be described in this document as serial or dodecaphonic--for the sake of simplicity.

[2]The dates of documents listed in this selected annotated bibliography range from 1934 through 1987-1988.

[3]The documents listed in this selected annotated bibliography are much taken up with issues which seem to be of great importance to the present author: the explication of theoretical and/or compositional aspects of the music of Italian serial composers. As such, interviews, musical critiques and analyses, stylistic surveys, biographies, and listings of compositions contribute to a projection of

were actually used. These cards were shuffled alphabetically (i. e. by composer and article) to order the bibliography into the Composer/Subject Index. Annotated books and/or articles which refer to more than one Italian serial composer in that index are listed under the Italian Dodecaphony heading. Reference to a specific Italian serial composer (individually or in a group with several non-Italian serial composers or non-Italian composers) in a book and/or article designates a listing under the heading of the corresponding composer.

An additional feature of this bibliography is the inclusion of several other indexes: an Author/Editor Index, a Periodical/Journal Index, and a Book Publisher Index. Thus, reference lists of scholars, publications, and publishers contributing to much of the current knowledge on Italian serial music and the Italian avant-garde are provided.

Special thanks is given to Drs. Dale J. Bonge, Rosalie Schellhous, and Conrad Donakowski for their help and assistance in this project. Also, the kindness of Charlotte, my wife, is lovingly appreciated. Such prolonged labor could not have been accomplished without her.

Harvey J. Stokes
September, 1989

---

this knowledge to interested musicians. On the other hand, reviews of performances of compositions (other than those listed in this document), for example, tend to avoid issues of theoretical and/or compositional importance. Thus, their exclusion from this document seems appropriate.

ABBREVIATIONS

+	article contained on later pages of issue
ed.	edition
edit.	editor(s)
MA 4-6	page numbers 4-6 in the *Musical America* section of the *High Fidelity/Musical America* journal
n.	number
n. a.	no author given
n. d.	no data given
n. p.	no publisher given
n. ppg.	no page numbers given
n. v.	no volume number given
p.	page
sect.	section
supp.	supplement
germ.	German
trans.	translated

DA-221 A representative entry identification mark; initially used in **I. Composer/Subject Index**. The letters represent the composer or subject discussed in the article or book of the entry (they are the initial letters of the *last* name of the specific composer, and the first two letters of the subject **Italian Dodecaphony**). The number to the right of the dash is the specific number of the 478 total entries.

I. COMPOSER/SUBJECT INDEX

BERIO, LUCIANO

BE-1   Albera, P. "Materiau et composition; sur trois oeuvres vocales de Luciano Berio," *Canadian University Music Review* n. 4 (1983): 66-94.
            Compositions discussed at some length include *Circles, O King,* and *Sequenza III.*

BE-2   Altmann, P. *Sinfonia von Luciano Berio -- eine analytische Studie.* Vienna: Universal, 1977.
            The composition *Sinfonia* by Luciano Berio is discussed at length from an analytical viewpoint. Musical examples and diagrams abound. This is an important study of one of Berio's most intriguing works.

BE-3   Anhalt, I. "Luciano Berio's *Sequenza III*," *Canadian Music Book* 7 (Autumn-Winter 1973): 23-60.
            An analysis of the composition *Sequenza III* by Berio. Included in this thesis is a summary of the article in French, and a wealth of musical examples.

BE-4   Bachmann, C. H. "Ein Neuer Name," *Zeitschrift für Musik* 116 (March 1955): 180.
            Variations for Orchestra, a work by Berio, is discussed succinctly in regard to inherent dodecaphonic activity.

BE-5   Barzetti, M. "Luciano Berio: a well-tempered composer," *Musical Events* 19 (Feb. 1964): 6-8.
            The article describes Berio's compositional psychology as well as his usage of the twelve-tone technique.

BE-6   Beckwith, John, and Kasemets, Udo, edit. *The Modern Composer and His World.* Toronto: University of Toronto Press, 1961.

BE-7   Berio, Luciano. "Eroismo electronico," *Nuova Rivista Musicale Italiana* 6, n. 4 (1972): 673-665.

BE-8   _____. *Luciano Berio: Two Interviews.* Trans. and Edit. by D. Osmond-Smith. London: Marian Boyars, 1985.
         Eight interviews are here; the compositional activity and ideology of Berio is discussed thereby. The interviewers are Bálint András Varga and Rossana Dalmonte.

BE-9   _____. "Meditation über ein Zwölftone-Pferd," *Melos* 36 (1968): 293-295.
         Berio discusses his dodecaphonic ideology.

BE-10   _____. "Poesie e musica -- un esperienza," *Incontri Musicali* 3 (Aug. 1959): 98-111.
         This article addresses psychological and contextual similarities between pure musical utterance and the reading of poetry. H. K. Metzger has translated it for publication in *Darmstädter Beiträge zur Neuen Musik* 2: (1959) 36-45. Another journal containing Berio's article is *Revue Belge de Musicologie* 13, n. 1-4 (1959): 68-75.

BE-11   _____. "Sur la musique electronique," *Schweizerische Musikzeitung* 97 (June 1957): 265.

BE-12   Bosseur, J. Y. "Un centre de recherches aujourd'hui," *Revue d' Esthetique* 3-4 (1974): 388-389.

BE-13   Braun, W. R. "Three Uses of Pre-Existant Music in the Twentieth-Century," *Dissertation Abstracts* 36 (May 1976): 7033A.
         The author locates and discusses usages of older musical elements (quodlibets, cantus firmi, etc.) in contemporary compositions; among works discussed is the composition *Sinfonia* by Berio.

BE-14   Brindle, R. S. "Broadcasting," *Musical Times* 103: 174-175.

BE-15   _____. "Italy," *Musical Times* 98 (Jan. 1957): 39.

BE-16 _____. "Italy," *Musical Quarterly* 44 (Jan. 1958): 95-101.
The composition *Nones* by Berio is discussed.

BE-17 Bristiger, M. *"Circles* -- Luciano Berio," *Ruch Muzyczny* 7, n. 22 (1963): 10-11.

BE-18 "CAPAC-MacMillan Lectures -- July 29, 30 (also in French)," *Canadian Composer* n. 101 (May 1975): 28-29.
The article addresses information given by Luciano Berio at the MacMillan lectures. Included in this article is a biography of the composer.

BE-19 Cadieu, M. "La memoire et les songes," *Musique en Jeu* n. 29 (Nov. 1977): 23-34.

BE-20 Chapin, L. "The Future Started Here," *Broadcast Music Inc.* (Summer 1970): p. 27-28.
A biography is included with an exposé of the career of Luciano Berio.

BE-21 Dalmonte, Rossana, editor. *Il gesto della forma: musica, poesia, teatro nell'opera di Luciano Berio.* Milan: Arcadia, 1981.
A collection of articles which discuss analytically several aspects of the following vocal works of Berio: *Passaggio, Laborintus II, Epifanie,* and *Sequenza III.* Authors of the articles include N. Lorenzini, L. Azzaroni, and F. Frasnedi. A review of the book is provided by Michael Eckert in *Journal of Music Theory* 27, n. 1 (1983): 140-145.

BE-22 _____. *Luciano Berio: entretiens avec Rossana Dalmonte.* Trans. by M. Kaltnecker. Paris: Lattes, 1983.

BE-23 D'Amico, F. "Campane a sera," *Nuova Rivista Musicale Italiana* 4 (Sept.-Oct. 1970): 910-912.

BE-24 Deliege, C. "L'invenzione musicale contemporanea (tentativo di sintesi)," *Nuova Rivista Musicale Italiana* 4, n. 4-5 (1970): 637-664, 880-897.

BE-25 DeRhen, A. "Berio at the Whitney," *High Fidelity/Musical America* 20 July 1970): 18-19, sec. 2.

BE-26   Donat, M. "Berio and his *Circles*," *Musical Times* 105 (Feb. 1964):
           105, 107
                     The composition *Circles* is discussed and critiqued
           analytically. A musical excerpt is included as well.

BE-27   Donovalova, V. "Nove funcie slova v hudbe -- v suvislosti s
           niektorymi vyvojorymi tendenciami sucasneho umenia,"
           Musicologia Slovaca 5 (1974): 221-275.
                     A summary of the article is given in German.

BE-28   Dressen, N. *Sprache und Musik bei Luciano Berio; Untersuchungen zu
           seinen Volkompositionen.* Regensburg: G. Bosse, 1982.
                     The book addresses several aspects of Berio's vocal
           works. A book review is provided by Marita Einemann in
           Neue Zeitschrift für Musik n. 7-8 (Jul., Aug 1983): 68.

BE-29   Duerr, B. "Journal des 'Chants Parallels' de Luciano Berio," *La Revue
           Musicale* n. 394-397 (1986): 72-73.

BE-30   Emmerson, S. "Luciano Berio," *Music and Musicians* 24 (Feb. 1976):
           26-28.
                     An interview with the composer on his music;
           present compositional trends are discussed along with his
           compositional ideology. The composer's portrait is included.

BE-31   _____. "Reich and Berio," *Music and Musicians* 24 (June 1977):
           58-59.
                     A discussion and critique of each composer's
           compositional output and work.

BE-32   _____. "Xenakis and Berio," *Music and Musicians* 24 (June 1976):
           53-54.
                     A discussion and critique of each composer's
           compositional output and work.

BE-33   Felder, D. "An Interview with Luciano Berio," *The Composer (U. S.)*
           7, n. 16 (1975-76): 9-15.

BE-34   Flynn, W. "Listening to Berio's Music," *Musical Quarterly* 61, n. 3
           (1975) :388-421.
                     A very informative and important critique of the
           music of Berio; suggestions as to how to listen to these
           compositions are offered as well. Analyses of several works

are present, as well as many illustrations and musical examples. A portrait of the composer is also included.

BE-35   Foertig, P. "Zu Luciano Berios *Sequenza* per oboe solo," *Tibia* n. 2 (1976): 72-76.

BE-36   Hamilton, D. "European Pioneers of the New Music," *High Fidelity/Musical America* 18 (Sept. 1968): 51.

BE-37   Hicks, M. "Text, Music, and Meaning in the Third Movement of Luciano Berio's *Sinfonia*," *Perspectives of New Music* 20, n. 1-2 (1981-1982): 199-224.
         An article which attempts to address psychic musical elements in movement III of *Sinfonia*.

BE-38   Holmes, R. K. "Relational Systems and Process in Recent Works of Luciano Berio." *Dissertation Abstracts* 42 (Jan 1982): 2924A.
         An analysis which shows how various compositional techniques and parameters of music are used to obtain "formal" shape on different levels. Works analyzed are *Sincronic* (1964), *Chemins II su Sequenza VI* (1969), *Concerto for Two Pianos* (1973), and *Points on the Curve to Find* (1974).

BE-39   Jahnke, S. "Materialien zu einer Unterrichts-sequenz 'Des Antonius von Padua Fischpredigt' bei Orff -- Mahler -- Berio," *Musik und Bildung* 5: 615-622..
         The composition discussed under "Berio" is *Sinfonia*.

BE-40   Jarvlepp, J. "Compositional Aspects of *Tempi Concertati* by Luciano Berio," *Interface/Journal of New Music Research* 11, n. 4 (1982): 179-93.

BE-41   "Journees de Musique Contemporaine de Paris 25-31 Oct. 1968," *the entire issue of La Revue Musicale* n. 267 (1969).

BE-42   Koch, G. R. "Musiksprach -- Sprachmusik, der Komponist Luciano Berio," *HIFI/Stereophonie* 10 (Dec. 1971): 1143-1146+.

BE-43   Konold, W. "Musik zwischen sprach und aktion -- einige Aspekte zun Schaffen von Luciano Berio," *Musica* 25, n. 5 (1971): 453-457.

BE-44   _____. "Schallplatten: Werk von Luciano Berio," *Musica* 25, n. 5
             (1971): 518.

BE-45   Krieger, G., and Stroh, W. M. "Probleme der Collage in der Musik
             aufgezeigt am 3. Satz der *Sinfonia* von Luciano Berio," *Musik
             und Bildung* 3 (May 1971): 229-235.

BE-46   Kropfinger, Klaus. "Lautfelder und Kompositorisches Gefüge bei
             Luciano Berio," *Darmstädter Beiträge zur Neuen Musik* n. 14
             (1974): 45-58.

BE-47   Lamb, M. L. "The Musical, Literary, and Graphic Influences upon
             Luciano Berio's *Thema, Omaggio a Joyce*," *Dissertation
             Abstracts* 38 (April 1978): 5789-90A.
                     A "musique concrete" composition (Berio's *Thema,
             Omaggio a Joyce*) is discussed at to its musical, literary, and
             graphic influences. An exceedingly informative study in 190
             pages.

BE-48   "Le interviste di Luciano Berio," *Nuova Rivista Musicale Italiana* 14, n.
             1 (1980): 98-99, n. a.
                     One of many interviews with the composer;
             discussed topics include twelve-tone ideology as well as
             compositional psychology.

BE-49   "Luciano Berio," *Nutida Musik* 12, n. 2 (1968-1969): 13, n. a.
                     Biographical information is given.

BE-50   "Luciano Berio," *Santa Cecilia* 11 (Apr. 1962): 43, n. a.
                     Biographical information is given, as well as a list of
             compositions.

BE-51   Mann, R. E. "Pitch Structure and Poetic Imagery in Luciano Berio's
             Wasserklavier and *Erdenklavier*," *Dissertation Abstracts* 47
             (July 1986): 15A.
                     The Berio works *Wasserklavier* (1965) and
             Erdenklavier (1969) and analyzed as to pitch structure as well
             as to connections which may exist between the poetic subject
             matter and the music.

BE-52   Mazurek, R. C. "Compositional Procedures in Selected Woodwind
             Quintets as Commissioned by the Dorian Quintet,"
             Dissertation Abstracts 47 (Mar 1987): 3234A.

Of several examined compositions, the Berio work *Children's Play for Wind Quintet: Opus Number Zoo* is of interest.

BE-53   Miller, R. W. "A Style of the Published Solo Piano Music of Luciano Berio," *Dissertation Abstracts* 40 (Oct. 1979): 1742A.
ι   Works studied include *Wasserkklavier* (c. 1971), *Erdenklavier* (c. 1971), *Cinque Variationi* (c. 1954, rev. c. 1969), *Rounds* (c. 1968), and *Sequenza IV* (c. 1967). Musical analysis is accomplished by an exploration of several parameters (pitch, texture, harmony, dynamics, range, meter, rhythm, tempo, and special effects).

BE-54   Nilsson, A. "Etapper i Luciano Berios muskskapande," *Musikrevy* 40, n.6 (1985): 233-234+.

BE-55   Noergaard, H. "Berio paa scenen 1981," *Dansk Musiktidsskrift* 55, n. 4 (1981): 187-189.

BE-56   Osmond-Smith, D. "Berio and the Art of Commentary," *Musical Times* 116 (Oct. 1975): 871-872.

BE-57   _____. "From Myth to Music: Levi-Strauss's *Mythologiques* and Berio's *Sinfonia*," *Musical Quarterly* 67, n. 2 (1981): 230-260.
         An extensive and important article; crucial to the understanding of several aspects of Berio's *Sinfonia*. Abundant musical examples are here, as well as informative discourse.

BE-58   _____. *Playing On Words: A Guide to Luciano Berio's Sinfonia*. Cambridge: Royal Musical Association, 1985.
         A significant contribution to knowledge on Berio's *Sinfonia*. A review is offered by Mike Smith in *Tempo* n. 153 (June 1985): 42-43.

BE-59   Orga, A. "20th-Century Masters," *Musical Events* 28 (Apr. 1973): 20-22+.
         A biography of Luciano Berio is given.

BE-60   Pellman, S. F. "An Examination of the Role of Timbre in a Musical Composition as Exemplified by an Analysis of *Sequenza V* by Luciano Berio," *Dissertation Abstracts* 401 (May. 1980): 4794A.

An examination of the role of timbre in *Sequenza V*
by Berio. Score study and careful listening was used to obtain
data in this analysis.

BE-61   Petersen, G. "Luciano Berio: Stockholm,." *Tonfallet* n. 1: 4-5 (Jan.
          18, 1980).
               Another interview with the composer.

BE-62   Petri, H. "Identatät von Sprache und Musik," *Melos* 32 (Oct. 1965):
          347-348.
               Berio's *Thema, Omaggio a Joyce* is discussed.

BE-63   Pinzauti, L. "Ich sprach mit Luciano Berio," *Melos* 37 (May 1970):
          177-181.
               An interview with the composer; comments on
          compositional ideology abound.

BE-64   Pousseur, H. "Calculation and Imagination in Electronic Music,"
          Electronic Music Review n. 5 (Jan. 1968): 21-29.

BE-65   Prieberg, Fred K. "Imajinäres Gespräch mit Luciano Berio," *Melos* 32
          (May 1965): 156-165.
               An extensive and informative interview with Berio
          on his music and ideology. Music examples are everywhere
          present, as well as portraits of Berio and Cathy Berberian.

BE-66   Rands, B. "The Master of New Sounds," *Music and Musicians* 19
          (Aug. 1971): 32-36, 38-40.
               An exceedingly broad article tracing the historical
          development of Berio's compositional legacy. It includes
          several photos of Berio, a single photo of Cathy Berberian,
          and an excerpt from *Black is the Color*, one of several Berio
          compositions.

BE-67   Rittelmeyer, C. "Zur Auswirkung der Prestige suggestion auf die
          Beuteilung der Neuen Musik," *Musik und Bildung* 3 (Feb.
          1971): 72-74.

BE-68   Roth, D. "Luciano Berio on New Music," *Musical Opinion* 99 (Sept.
          1976): 548-549, 551.
               An interview with the composer on his serial
          ideology and work at IRCAM.

BE-69   Sams, C. L. "Solo Vocal Writing in Selected Works of Berio, Crumb, and Rochberg," *Dissertation Abstracts* 37 (Aug. 1976): 685A.
             Specific aspects of progressive tendencies in the vocal writing of Berio, Crumb, and Rochberg are given. Biographies are offered initially, the vocal study ensues thereafter.

BE-70   Santi, Piero. "Luciano Berio," *Young Composers -- Die Reihe* 4 (Bryn Mawr, 1960 -- germ. ed. 1958): 98-102.
             A critique of the compositional procedure and ideology of Luciano Berio. The article is quite informative; it reveals much that is essential to an understanding of Berio's music.

BE-71   Sayler, B. "Looking Backward: Reflections on Nostalgia in the Avant-Garde," *Centerpoint* 1, n. 3 (1975): 5.
             Berio's composition *Sinfonia* is discussed (among works by other composers).

BE-72   Schibli, Sigfried. "Schillernd Virtuos und auch al Lehrer attraktiv: Eine Woche mit Luciano Berio an der Musik-Academie in Basel," *Neue Zeitschrift für Musik* n. 4 (Apr. 1986): 48-49.
             Reflections on the workshop given by Berio in Basel.

BE-73   Schnaus, P. "Anmerkungen zu Luciano Berio's *Circles*," *Musik und Bildung* 10 (July-Aug. 1978): 489-497.

BE-74   Schneerson, G. "Die musikalische 'Avant-garde' der sechziger Jahre," *Musik und Gesellschaft* 21. (Dec. 1971): 754-760.

BE-75   Schulman, M. "Luciano Berio 1975: Speech and Music Revisited, " *Canadian Composer* n. 103 (Sept. 1975): 18-19.

BE-76   Schwartz, E. "Current Chronicle: The Netherlands Festival," *Musical Quarterly* 58, n. 4 (1972): 653-658.
             An analytic discussion of several Berio compositions performed at a festival in the Netherlands.

BE-77   Sjoeberg, L. "Med verkligheten foer oeronen -- om Luciano Berio," *Nutida Musik* 16, n. 4 (1972-73): 23-27.

BE-78   Soria, D. J. "Artist Life," *High Fidelity/Musical America* 20 (July 1970): 4-5, sect. 2.

BE-79   Stoianova, I. "Luciano Berio, chemins en musique," *the entire issue of La Revue Musicale* n. 375-377 (1985).

BE-80   Tassone, P. S. "The Musical Language in Luciano Berio's *Points on the Curve to Find,*" *Dissertation Abstracts* 48 (Oct. 1987): 777A.
An ample analysis of the Berio work *Points on the Curve to Find.*

BE-81   Thomas, J. "Contemporary Music and the Avant-Garde: An Introduction," *Organist Review* 69, n. 279 (1985): 37-38.

BE-82   Tykesson, A. "Droemmens aaterkomst: om Luciano Berio och hans cellokonsert," *Nutida Musik* 31, n. 1 (1987-1988): 30-33.

BE-83   Uscher, Nancy. "Luciano Berio: *Sequenza VI for Solo Viola:* Performance Practices," *Perspectives of New Music* 21 n. 1-2 (1982-1983): 286-293.
Significant discourse on various aspects of performing this Berio composition.

BE-84   "Varese -- Xenakis -- Berio -- Pierre Henry: Oeuvres, Etudes, Perspectives," the entire issue of *La Revue Musicale* n. 265-266 (1969).

BE-85   Vermeulen, E. "Berio in Rotterdam," *Mens en Melodie* 34 (Mar. 1979): 68-76.

BE-86   Zillig, Winfried. *Variationen über Neue Musik.* Munich: Nymphenburger, 1959.

BE-87   Zijlstra, M. "Het componeren van de avant-garde in de Zoste eeuw," *Mens en Melodie* 31 (Jan. 1976): 5.

BE-88   Zupko, R. "Darmstadt: New Directions," *Perspectives of New Music* 2, n. 2 (1964): 166-169.
Seminars at Darmstädt were reviewed in this article; the Berio lecture "Instrument and Function" is of importance.

BUSSOTTI, SYLVANO

BU-89   Bramble, R. "Sweden," *Opera* 20 (Jan. 1969): 64-66.

BU-90   Bussotti, Sylvano. *I miei teatri, diario segreto, diario pubblico, alcuni saggi*. Palermo: Novecento, 1982. Reviewed in *Nuova Rivista Musicale Italiana* 19, n. 2 (1985): 320-321.

BU-91   Fleuret, M. "Sylvano Bussotti -- une musique dans la musique," *La Revue Musicale* n. 276-277 (1971): 11-14.

BU-92   Gallarati, P. "Da Torino," *Nuova Rivista Musicale Italiana* 11, n. 2 (1977): 242-243.

BU-93   Goebels, F. "Gestalt und Gestaltung musikalisher Grafik," *Melos* 39, n. 1 (1972): 23-34.

BU-94   Gould, S. "Florence," *Opera* 26 (May 1975): 478-480.

BU-95   Haglund, R. "Bussotti och romantikens aater komst," *Musikrevy* 35, n. 4-5 (1980): 166+.

BU-96   "Journees de musique contemporaine -- Paris 19-27 Octobre 1970," *La Revue Musicale* n. 270-271 (1971): 17-25, *Schweizersche Musikzeitung* 111, n. 2 (1971): 108-109.

BU-97   Jungheinrich, H. K. "Zeremoniemeister des Larters," *Opern Welt* 3 (Mar. 1969): 34-37.

BU-98   Maehder, J. *Bussottioperaballet*: Sviluppi della drammaturgia musicale bussottiana," *Nuova Rivista Musicale Italiana* 18, n. 3 (1984): 441-468.

BU-99   Mandelli, A. "Bastian contrari (e falci fienale)," *Rassegna Musicale Curci* 30, n. 2 (1977): 13-16.

BU-100   Morini, L., and Premoli, A. *Träume in Samt und Seide: Mystik und Realitaet in den Opernkostumen des Sylvano Bussotti.* Munich: Flade & Partner, 1985.
         A review can be located in *Musica* 40, n. 5 (1986): 466.

BU-101   Neufert, K. "Interview," *Opera Welt* 28, n. 3 (1987): 12-13.
         An interview with Sylvano Bussotti.

BU-102   Oehlschlaegal, R. "Mixed Media, Collage, und Montage," *Opern Welt* 3 (Mar. 1969): 38-39.

BU-103   Piamonte, G. "Da Milano," *Nuova Rivista Musicale Italiana* 10, n. 2 (1976): 268-274.
         A discussion of the Bussotti composition *Bussottioperaballet.*

BU-104   _____. "Ich interviewte Sylvano Bussotti, *Melos* 38 (Jul.-Aug. 1971): 284-291.
         An extensive interview with the composer about his compositional ideology. Musical examples are here, along with a portrait of Bussotti.

BU-105   Scherzer, E. "Sylvano Bussotti (ein Gespräch)," *Neue Zeitschrift für Musik* n. 4 (Apr. 1984): 17-18.
         An interview with the composer. A list of compositions and a photo is included.

BU-106   Schiffer, B. "Schallplatten -- The London Music Digest," *Melos* 41, n. 6 (1974): 385-395.
         The Bussotti compositions *Pertre'sul Piano* and *Pour Piano* are discussed. A biography of the composer is included.

BU-107   "Sylvano Bussotti," *Nutida Musik* 12, n. 2 (1968)-1969): 30.

A biography of the life and musical activity of Sylvano Bussotti is provided.

BU-108   Urmetzer, R. "Mehr als nur Musik: ein Seminar mit Sylvano Bussotti in Stuttgart," *Neue Zeitschrift für Musik* n. 4 (Apr. 1986): 46-47.

BU-109   Vermeulen, E. "Festival nieuwe muziek van Jeugd en Muziek Zeeland," *Mens en Melodie* 33 (Oct. 1978): 320-332.

BU-110   Vogt, Matthias. "Komponieren in Möglichkeitsform: Sylvano Bussotti in Luxemburg," *Neue Zeitschrift für Musik* n. 6 (June 1985): 37-38.

CASTIGLIONI, NICCOLO

CA-111   Bortolotto, M. "Om Niccolo Castiglioni," *Nutida Musik* 9, n. 1-2 (1965-1966); 31-36.
Musical examples are present along with a critique of compositional procedure and style. A portrait of the composer is included also.

CA-112   Buck, O. "Niccolo Castiglioni, italiensk komponist: stoejen goer ikke godt, de gode goer ikke stoej," *Dansk Musiktidsskrift* 56, n. 5 (1981-1982): 196+.
A discography is provided as well as much discussion about the composer and his many accomplishments.

CA-113   Campo, F. "Report from Venice (1982)," *Perspectives of New Music* 21, n. 1-2 (1982-1983): 376.
Among the music of other composers, the premier of *Sacro Concerto* by Castiglioni is of analytic interest.

CA-114   Castiglioni, Niccolo. "Gli Study," *Musica d'Oggi* 3 (Jul. 1960): 327-330.

CA-115   _____. *Il linguaggio musicale dal Rinascimento ad Oggi.* Milan: Ricordi, 1959.
A review is contained in the periodical *Musica d' Oggi.*

CA-116   "Richieste dall Accademia di Santa Cecilia quàtro composizioni sinfoniche da presentare in prima esccuzione," *Santa Cecilia* 11 (Apr. 1962): 21-23, n. a.
Biographical information is given on Niccolo Castiglioni.

1 4

CA-117   "Voci aggiunte e rivedute per un dizionario di compositori viventi," *La Rassegna Musicale* 31, n. 1 (1961): 46-47, n. a.
A succinct biography on Castiglioni is given along with a listing of compositions from 1956 to 1960.

CLEMENTI, ALDO

CL-118   Bortolotto, M. "Aldo Clementi," *Melos* 30 (Nov. 1963): 364-369.
          A most important article on the musical legacy of
          Aldo Clementi. Several compositions are analyzed, with
          an abundance of musical examples and illustrations.

CL-119   "Clementi, Aldo," *Schweizerische Musikzeitung* 97 (June 1957):
          237-238, n. a.
          A biography of Aldo Clementi is given, along
          with a discussion of his *Sonata* for trumpet, guitar, and
          piano.

CL-120   Kohn, Karl. "Current Chronicle: L. A.," *Musical Quarterly* 50 (July
          1964): 370-371.
          The Clementi composition *Triplum* is analyzed
          succinctly. No musical examples are given.

CL-121   Muggler, F. "Bern und Zuerich wagen Experimente," *Melos* 37
          (Nov. 1970): 471.
          The work *Silben* by Clementi is discussed.

DALLAPICCOLA, LUIGI

DA-122   Annabaldi, C. "Dallapiccola e l'avant guardia 'impegnata'," *Quaderni della Rassegna Musicale* 2 (1965): 79-89.

DA-123   Alberti, L. "Dallapiccola attraverso i suoi scritti," *Quaderni della Rassegna Musicale* 2 (1965): 91-116.

DA-124   Ballo, F. "Le musiche corali di Dallapiccola," *La Rassegna Musicale* 10 (April 1937): 136-141.
Compositional genius in vocal music is discussed through an investigation of style traits in the output of Dallapiccola. A very important literary critique of his music.

DA-125   Baron, C. K. "The Composer as Poet: Meaning in the Music of Luigi Dallapiccola (1904-1975)," *Centerpoint* 1, n. 4 (1975-1976): 37-44.

DA-126   Basart, Ann P. "The Twelve-Tone Compositions of Luigi Dallapiccola," Unpublished Master's Thesis, University of California: Berkeley, 1960.

DA-127   Bialosky, M. "Remembering Dallapiccola," *American Society of University Composers* 11-12 (1978-1979): 86-93.

DA-128   "Bibliographie -- Luigi Dallapiccola," *Schweizerische Musikzeitung* 115, n. 4 (1975): 209-211, n. a.

DA-129   Borris, S. "Ein Hymniker der Liberta -- zum Tode Luigi Dallapiccolas," *Musik und Bildung* 7 (May 1975): 260-261.

DA-130   Boyd, Malcolm. "'Dies Irae': Some Recent Manifestations," *Music and Letters* 49, n. 4 (1968): 347-356.

Among other works, the *Canti di Prigionia* of Dallapiccola is discussed analytically as to its "Dies Irae" manifestations.

DA-131   Brachtel, K. R., "Angst und Hoffnung -- auf und zu," *Neue Zeitschrift für Musik* n. 10 (Oct. 1984): 31-32.
          The composition *Job* by Dallapiccola is mentioned.

DA-132   Brandt, M. "Is de tijd a rijp voor dit meesterwerk? De diepte-psychologie van Dallapiccola's *Ulysse*," *Mens en Melodie* 42 (Oct. 1987): 445-553.

DA-133   Brindle, Reginald Smith. "Current Chronicle -- Italy," *Musical Quarterly* 41 (Oct. 1955): 524-526.
          The composition *Marsia* by Dallapiccola is discussed. Musical examples are also included.

DA-134   _____. "Current Chronicle: Italy," *Musical Quarterly* 43 (Apr. 1957): 240-245.
          Choral music composed by Luigi Dallapiccola is discussed; musical examples are included.

DA-135   _____. "Italy," *Musical Times* 8 (Apr. 1957): 217-218.

DA-136   _____. "La fecnica corale di Luigi Dallapiccola," *Quaderni della Rassegna Musicale* 2 (1965): 47-48.

DA-137   Brown, Rosemary. "Continuity and Recurrence in the Creative Development of Luigi Dallapiccola," Ph.D. dissertation, University College of North Wales, 1977.

DA-138   _____. "La sperimentazione ritmica in Dallapiccola Tra liberta e determinazione," *Rivista Italiana di Musicologia* 13, n. 1 (1978): 142-173.

DA-139   Brunner, P. "Der Melodiker im Zwoelftonreich -- Zum Tod von Luigi Dallapiccola," *Musica* 29, n. 2 (1975): 160-161.
          Reflections on the varied accomplishments of the "melodic" serialist Luigi Dallapiccola.

DA-140   Buccheri, John. S. "An Approach to Twelve-tone Music: Articulation of Serial Pitch Units in Piano Works of Schoenberg, Webern,

Krenek, Dallapiccola, and Rochberg," *Dissertation Abstracts* 37 (Aug. 1976): 697A.

The composition (among others) *Quaderno Musicale di Annalibera* is discussed; the author is concerned with procedures whereby serial pitch units are articulated through non-pitch elements.

DA-141 Burt, F. "An Anthesis: The Aesthetic Aspect," *Score and IMA Magazine* n. 19 (Mar. 1957): 62-63.

DA-142 Connolly, J. "A Note on Luigi Dallapiccola," *Royal College of Music* 56, n. 3 (1960): 70-72.

DA-143 Dallapiccola, Luigi. "A Composer's Problem," *Opera* 12 (Jan. 1961): 8-11.

DA-144 _____. *Appunti, inconrti, meditazioni.* Milan: Suvini Zerboni, 1970.

A collection of letters, programme-notes, etc. written by Dallapiccola. The book also contains a bibliography of published and unpublished writings. Reviews can be found in *Melos* 38 (Oct. 1971): 420, and *Rivista Musicale Italiana* 5 (Jan.-Feb. 1971): 137-139. The document listed under *DA-146* is the enlargement of this book.

DA-145 _____. "On the Twelve-Note Road," *Music Survey* 4 (Oct. 1951): 318-332.

Dallapiccola makes valuable comments on the dodecaphonic process as he sees it and as used in his compositions. Despite the author's insistence to the contrary, the article is somewhat autobiographical.

DA-146 _____. *Parole e musica.* Milan: Saggiatore,1980.

An enlargement on the material listed under *DA-144*. A review is provided by Christopher Shaw in *Tempo* 138 (Sept. 1981): 45-46.

DA-147 _____. "Text et musique dans le melodrame (1961-1969)," *Musique en Jeu* n. 21 (Nov. 1975): 42-65.

The article occurred initially (in Italian) in *Quaderni Della Rassegna Musicale* 2 (1965 [L'Opera di Luigi Dallapiccola]): 117-139.

DA-148   _____. "The Genesis of the *Canti di Prigionia* and *Il Prigioniero*,"
              trans. by Jonathan Schiller, *Musical Quarterly* 39 (1953):
              355-372.
                      An autobiographical article which discusses the
              creation of acknowledged masterworks. An understanding of
              these compositions is made easier through this article.

DA-149   Damerini, A. "Con l'allieuo e col docente nel Conservatorio Cherubini
              de Firenze," *Quaderni della Rassegna Musicale* 2 (1965):
              71-77.

DA-150   D'Amico, F. "*Canti di Prigionia*," *Societa* 1 (1945), n. ppg.
                      Reflections on the Dallapiccola composition.

DA-151   _____. "Liberatione e prigionia," *I casi della Musica* (1962), n. v.,
              n. ppg.

DA-152   _____. "Luigi Dallapiccola," *Melos* 20 (March 1953): 69-74.
                      A critique of Dallapiccola's compositional activity
              and practice. Included are musical examples as well as a
              portrait of the composer.

DA-153   _____. "Recension -- Luigi Dallapiccola," *La Rassegna Musicale*
              17 (Apr. 1947): 165-170.

DA-154   Dapogny, J. E. "Style and Method in Three Compositions of Luigi
              Dallapiccola," *Dissertation Abstracts* 32 (Feb. 1972): 4648A.
                      Three Dallapiccola compositions are discussed as to
              compositional technique and structure: the *Goethe-Lieder*
              (1953), *Cinque Canti* (1956), and *Preghiere* (1962).

DA-155   DeBlonay, A. "Luigi Dallapiccola," *La Radio* (Lossana 1934), n. ppg.

DA-156   DeLio, T. "A Proliferation of Canons: Luigi Dallapiccola's *Goethe
              Lieder No. 2*," *Perspectives of New Music* 23, n. 2 (1985):
              186-195.
                      An interesting and informative analysis of the second
              song from Dallapiccola's *Goethe Lieder*. An abundance of
              musical examples are presented as well.

DA-157   _____. "A Proliferation of Canons II: Luigi Dallapiccola's *Goethe
              Lieder No. 6*," *Interface/Journal of New Music Research* 16,
              n. 1-2 (1987): 39+.

An analysis of the sixth song from Dallapiccola's *Goethe Lieder.*

DA-158 DePaoli, Domenico. "Chroniques et notes: Italie -- Luigi Dallapiccola," *La Revue Musicale* (Giugno 1935), n. ppg.

DA-159 _____. "An Italian Musician -- Luigi Dallapiccola," *Chesterian* 19 (1938): 157-163.
A favorable exposé of the young Dallapiccola and his music. There are no musical examples.

DA-160 Dibelius, V. "Luigi Dallapiccola," *Melos* 31 (Mar. 1964): 81-87.
A discussion of Dallapiccola's music up to the 1950's. The article also contains a biography, musical examples, a portrait of the composer, and other illustrations.

DA-161 "Die Schriften Luigi Dallapiccolas -- eine Auswahl," *Schweizerische Musikzeitung* 115, n. 4 (1975): 207-208, n. a.

DA-162 Drew, D. "Dallapiccola," *New Statesman and Nations* 57 (1957): 363.

DA-163 Eckert, Michael. "Test and Form in Dallapiccola's *Goethe-Lieder*," *Perspectives of New Music* 17, n. 2 (1979): 98-111.
An analysis of the *Goethe-Lieder* of Dallapiccola, with emphasis on the relevance of the music with the text.

DA-164 _____. "Luigi Dallapiccola: Review of New Recordings," *Perspectives of New Music* 21, n. 1-2 (1982-1983), 410-416.
Reviews recordings (which also receive analytical critique) are Dallapiccola's Complete Piano Works (*L'Opera per Pianoforte*), *Canti di Liberazione, Three Questions with Two Answers*, and a fourth recording which includes *Cinque Canti* and *Rencesvals.*

DA-165 Englemann, Hans, U. "Dallapiccola's *Canti di Liberazione*," *Melos* 23 (1956): 73-76.

DA-166 Exton, J. "Luigi Dallapiccola, The Teacher," *Studies in Music* 9 (1975): 77-78.

DA-167 "Fatti principali della vita di Luigi Dallapiccola," *Quaderni della Rassegna Musicale* 2 (1965): 157-161, n. a.

DA-168   Gatti, Guido. M. "Luigi Dallapiccola," *Monthly Musical Record* 66
          (Feb. 1936), n. ppg.

DA-169   Gavenzzi, G. "Le musiche giovanili di Dallapiccola." Saggio del 1935:
          30 anni di musica, n. ppg. Milan: Ricordi, 1958.

DA-170   _____. "Studi su Dallapiccola." In *Musicisti di Europa*, n. ppg.
          Milan: Surini-Serboni, 1954.

DA-171   Golea, A. "Un compositeur *Engage* -- Luigi Dallapiccola," *Musique
          Disques* (1961), n. ppg.

DA-172   _____. "Liberté et tyrannie dans l'oeuvre de Luigi Dallapiccola." In
          Vingt ans de musique contemporaine, n. ppg. Paris: Seghers,
          1962.

DA-173   Gould, G. H. "A Stylistic Analysis of Selected Twelve-Tone Works by
          Luigi Dallapiccola," *Dissertation Abstracts* 25 (May 1965):
          6676.
                    An analysis of several twelve-tone compositions by
          Luigi Dallapiccola:
                    1. *Ciaccona, Intermezzo e Adagio* for cello (1945)
                    2. *Due Studi* for violin and piano (1946-1947)
                    3. *Quaderno Musicale di Annalibera* for piano
                       (1953)
                    4. *Variazioni* for orchestra (1953)
                    5. *Piccolo Musica Notturna* for chamber orchestra
                       (1954)
                    6. *Concerto per la Notte di Natale dell anno 1956*
                       for soprano and chamber orchestra (1956-1957).
          Parameters discussed include dodecaphonic procedures, form,
          melody, texture, rhythm, orchestration, and textual setting.
          The dissertation is broad and informative.

DA-174   Helm, E. "Luigi Dallapiccola in einem (unverœffentlichten) Gespräch,"
          Melos/Neue Zeitschrift für Musik 2, n. 6 (1976): 469-471.
                    A discussion of Dallapiccola's legacy as a composer
          for vocal forces ensues, and is followed with a critique of his
          twelve-tone methodology.

DA-175   Hennenberg, F. "Gedenkblatte für Luigi Dallapiccola (1904-1975),"
          Musik und Gesellschaft 34 (Mar. 1984): 146-147.

DA-176   Ignasheva, O. "L. Dallapikkola ob opere i o sebe," *Sovetskaya Muzyka* 6 (June 1983): 99-103.

DA-177   "Interu'yu s Luidzhi Dallapikkola," *Sovetskaya Muzyka* 32 (Apr. 1967): 129-131, n. a.
A short (but informative) interview with Luigi ,Dallapiccola.

DA-178   Kaemper, D. "Commiato -- Bemerkung zu Dallapiccolas letztem Werk," *Schweizerische Musikzeitung* 115, n. 4 (1975): 195-200.

DA-179   _____. *Gefangenschaft und Freiheit; Leben und Werk des Komponisten Luigi Dallapiccola.* Cologne: Gitarre & Laute, 1984.
An important retrospective of the life and work of Dallapiccola. A review is presented in *Musica* 39, n. 5 (1985):, 492.

DA-180   _____. *Luigi Dallapiccola, la vita e l'opera.* Trans. by L. Dallapiccola and S. Sablich. Florence, 1985, n. p.
A review is presented in *Sovetskaya Muzyka* 7 (July 1986): 117-119.

DA-181   _____. "Luigi Dallapiccola und die italienische Musik der Dreissiger Jahre," *Musikforschung* 36, n. 1 (1983 supp.): 158-167.

DA-182   _____. Review of *Style and Method in Three Compositions of Luigi Dallapiccola* by J. E. Dapogny. *Schweizerische Musikzeitung* 115, n. 4 (1975): 208-209.

DA-183   _____. "Uno squardo nell'officina gli schizzi e gli abbozzi del *Prigioniero* di Luigi Dallapiccola," *Nuova Rivista Musicale Italiana* 14, n. 2 (1980): 227-239.

DA-184   Kaufmann, H. "Dallapiccola in Graz," *Melos* 23 (June 1956): 177-178.

DA-185   Kay, N. "The Humanity of Dallapiccola," *Music and Musicians* 14 (Aug. 1966): 22-25.
A timely discussion of the "mild" twelve-tone ideology as exemplified in Dallapiccola's compositions.

DA-186   Krellmann, H. "Luigi Dallapiccola -- nie modische," *Musikhandel* 26, n. 3 (1975): 123.

DA-187   Leibowitz, Rene. "Luigi Dallapiccola," *L'Arche* 3 (1947): 23-28.

DA-188   "Luigi Dallapiccola," *La Rassegna Musicale* 20 (Jan. 1950) 40-41, n. a.
          A listing of the compositions of Luigi Dallapiccola up to 1950 is provided.

DA-189   "Luigi Dallapiccola," *Cahiers de la Musique* 2 (1938) 101-102, n. a.

DA-190   Magrill, S. M. "The Principle of Variation: A Study in the Selection of Differences with Examples from Dallapiccola, J. S. Bach, and Brahms," *Dissertation Abstracts* 43 (Jun. 1983): 3749A.
          The Dallapiccola work discussed here is his *Quaderno Musicale di Annalibera* (for piano).

DA-191   Mancini, D. L. "Form and Polarity in Late Works of Luigi Dallapiccola," *Dissertation Abstracts* 46 (Nov. 1985): 1123A.
          The Dallapiccola works analyzed as to their form and polarity include *Commiato, Preghiere*, and *Sicut Umbra*.

DA-192   _____. "Twelve-Tone Polarity in Late Works of Luigi Dallapiccola," *Journal of Music Theory* 30, n. 2 (1986): 203-224.
          An informative critique of 12-tone procedure in the works of Dallapiccola.

DA-193   Mantelli, A. "Ritratto di Dallapiccola," *Meridiano di Rome* (6/3/1938): n. ppg.

DA-194   Manzoni, G. "Luigi Dallapiccola," *Rivista Musical Chilena* 17 n. 85 (1963): 50-72.
          Reflections on the artistic legacy and music of Luigi Dallapiccola.

DA-195   _____. "Luigi Dallapiccola -- The Complete Works: A Catalogue," *Tempo* n. 116 (Mar. 1976): 2-19.
          A useful document; indispensable for any attempt to reflect on the compositional output of the serial master.

DA-196   Matthes, W. "Heimkehr zu sich selbst Oldenburgische Erstauffuehrung der Dallapiccola-Oper *Ulisse*," *Das Orchester* 28 (Sep. 1980): 733-734.

DA-197   Mayer, Tony. "Marseilles," *Opera* 37 (Mar. 1986): 320-322.
          Besides other performances, the Dallapiccola opera *Volo di Notti*, is critiqued.

DA-198   Mila, M. "L'incontro Henza-Dallapiccola," *La Rassegna Musicale* 27 (Dec. 1957): 301-308.
          Twelve-tone compositional techniques are discussed in the Dallapiccola work *A Mathilde*.

DA-199   _____. "Il neomadrigalismo della musica Italiana," *Chronache Musicale* (1959), n. ppg.

DA-200   Mizell, J. "Trends, Analysis, and Style of Specific Compositions by 20th-Century Composers," *Dissertation Abstracts* 33 (Nov. 1972): 2415A.
          Tre Laude by Dallapiccola is discussed (among works by other composers) as to performance practices, text translations, and analytical findings.

DA-201   Montagu, G. "Luigi Dallapiccola," *London Musical Events* 11 (May 1956): 27+.

DA-202   Morton, L. *"Canti Di Prigionia,"* *Counterpoint* (Feb. 1953), n. ppg.

DA-203   Nathan, Hans. "Considerations sur la maniere de travailler de Luigi Dallapiccola," *Schweizerische Musikzeitung* 115, n. 4 (1975): 180-193.
          A most important "sketchbook" describing the compositional processes of the dodecaphonic master. Musical examples abound in the article. An English translation of this article appears in *Perspectives of New Music* 15, n. 2 (1977): 34-51.

DA-204   _____. "Luigi Dallapiccola: Fragments from Conversations," *Music Review* 27, n. 4 (1966): 294-312.
          Hans Nathan provides a "collage" of different segments of interviews with Luigi Dallapiccola. Musical examples are given in correspondence with responses made by Dallapiccola's to Nathan's questions.

DA-205   _____. "The Twelve-Tone Compositions of Luigi Dallapiccola,"
                Musical Quarterly 44 (July, 1958): 289-310.
                        The article begins with a synopsis of the
                dodecaphonic procedure as practiced by the Viennese masters.
                A subsequent synopsis of the twelve-tone works of
                Dallapiccola is provided through an investigation of melody,
                harmony, and rhythm. After a consideration of Dallapiccola's
                motivation for dodecaphony, the article concludes with an
                assessment of the composer's importance in the history of
                music as well as a complete list of the twelve-tone works.

DA-206   Nicoldi, F., "Luigi Dallapiccola e la Scuola di Vienna: considerzioni e
                note in margine a un a scelta," *Rivista Musicale Italiana* 17, n.
                3-4 (1983): 493+.

DA-207   _____, edit. *Luigi Dallapiccola -- saggi, testimonianze, carteggio,
                biografia e bibliografia.* Milan: Suvini Zerboni, 1975.
                        One of the more important retrospective documents
                on Dallapiccola's life and work. Reviews are found in *Nuova
                Rivista Musicale Italiana* 10, n. 2 (1976): 288-289, and
                Schweizerische Musikzeitung 117, n. 3 (1977): 172.

DA-208   Paap, W. "Luigi Dallapiccola (1904-1975): componist, lettre en
                humanist," *Mens en Melodie* 30 (May 1975): 130-132.

DA-209   Perkins, J. M. "Dallapiccola's Art of Canon," *Perspectives of New
                Music* 1, n. 2 (1963): 95-106.

DA-210   Petrassi, G., Martino, D., Perkins, J., and Sessions, R. "In memoriam
                -- Luigi Dallapiccola," *Perspectives of New Music* 13 (1974):
                240-245.
                        Petrassi, Donald Martino, John Perkins, and Roger
                Sessions comment of the life and artistic legacy of
                Dallapiccola.

DA-211   Petrobelli, P. "Luigi Dallapiccola," *Musical Times* 116 (Apr. 1975):
                337-338.

DA-212   Petrucchi, G. "La dodecafonia di Dallapiccola," *L'Italia* (1950): 22-27.

DA-213   Pedrotti, A. "Luigi Dallapiccola," *Il Trentino* (Feb. 1936), n. ppg.

DA-214   Piccardi, C. "Luigi Dallapiccola -- a ragione Incatenata," *Schweizerische Musikzeitung* 115, n. 4 (1975): 169-171. A summary of this article is included in French.

DA-215   Pinzauti, L. "L'ereditá di Verdi nella condotta vocale del Prigioniero," *Quaderni della Rassegna Musicale* 2 (1965): 11-21.

DA-216   _____, edit. "Un inedito di Dallapiccola," *Nuova Rivista Musicale Italiana* 9, n. 2 (1975): 248-256.

DA-217   Qualliotine, G. "Extended Set Procedures in Two Compositions of Luigi Dallapiccola," *Dissertation Abstracts* 47 (Jan. 1987): 2365A.
       Analyses of pitch organization in the *Quaderno Musicale di Annalibera* and "Ritmi" from *Quattro Liriche di Antonio Machado.*

DA-218   Sabbe, H. "Luigi Dallapiccola -- het humanistisch buwustzijn in de modern muziek," *Mens en Melodie* 19 (Mar. 1964): 77-82.

DA-219   Santi, Piero. "Premessa allo studio dell' idea seriale in Schoenberg e in Dallapiccola," *Quaderni della Rassegna Musicale* 2 (1965): 59-65.

DA-220   Schweizer, G. "Luigi Dallapiccola -- eine Begegnung in Italien," *Neue Zeitschrift für Musik* 126 (Feb. 1965): 65-66.

DA-222   "Scritti su Luigi Dallapiccola," *Quaderni della Rassegna Musicale* 2 (1965): 151-153, n. a.

DA-223   Shackelford, R. "Dallapiccola e l'organo (not as by Vlad, R.--trans. from *Tempo* n. 111, Dec. 1974)," *Rivista Musicale Italiana* 9, n. 3 (1975): 367-381.
       The composition *Quaderno Musicale di Annalibera* is analyzed by Rudy Shackelford. The article is a by-product of Shackelford's arrangement of a Dallapiccola organ composition.

DA-224   _____, trans. "A Dallapiccola Chronology," *Musical Quarterly* 67, n. 3 (1981): 405-436.
       Mr. Shackelford has reprinted in translation this article from the book *Luigi Dallapiccola -- saggi, testimonianze, carteggio, biografia e bibliografia* (Nicoldi, F.,

edit., *DA-207*). It is a chronological listing of important events
in the life of Dallapiccola (1904-1975). Footnotes annotate the
events; informative information is thus here.

DA-225   Skulsky, A "Dallapiccola Felt Impelled to Introduce a New Romantic
           Era," *Musical America* (Mar 1949), n. ppg.

DA-226   _____. "L'oeuvre de Luigi Dallapiccola," *Cahiers de la Musique* 3
           (Bruxelles, 1939): 2-15.

DA-227   Stuckenschmidt, H. *Schöpfer der neuen Musik*. Frankfurt: Suhrkamp,
           1958.
                 Dallapiccola is discussed on pages 228-240.

DA-228   Ugolini, G. "*Il Prigioniero* di Luigi Dallapiccola," *La Rassegna
           Musicale* 32, n. 2 (1962): 233-241.
                 A discussion of the Dallapiccola opera *Il Prigioniero*.

DA-229   _____. "Vocalitá e dramma in Luigi Dallapiccola," *Quaderni della
           Rassegna Musicale* 2 (1965): 23-46.

DA-230   Varga, B. A. "Grazi beszelgetes Luigi Dallapiccolaval," *Muzsika* 16
           (Oct. 1973): 19-21.

DA-231   Varnai, P. *Beszelgetesek Luigi Dallapiccolaval*. Budapest:
           Zenemukiado, 1977.

DA-232   Vlad, Roman. "Luigi Dallapiccola," *Horizon* (decembre 1949, gennaio
           1950), n. ppg.

DA-233   _____. *Luigi Dallapiccola*. Milan: Suvini-Zerboni, 1957.
                 A chronological exposé of the artistic legacy of
           Dallapiccola. The author discusses that which he sees as quite
           unique in Dallapiccola's music: a fusion of diatonic and
           dodecaphonic procedure. Musical examples are abundant, and
           included with the text is a list of published work as well as
           biographical information. Review are provided in *Music and
           Letters* 39 (July 1958): 310-311, *Chesterian* 33 (1958):
           99-101, and *Musical Times* 100 (Feb. 1959): 84.

DA-234   _____. "Dallapiccola 1948-1966," *Score and IMA Magazine* 15
           (1956): 39-62.

DA-235   _____. "A footnote to Dallapiccola and the Organ," *Tempo* n. 116 (Mar. 1976): 21-23.
           This article is a defense against several alleged analytical mistakes ascribed to Vlad's book *Luigi Dallapiccola* by Rudy Shackleford in his *Dallapiccola and the Organ* (Dallapiccola e l'organo) article (see *DA-223*)

DA-236   _____. *Storio della Dodecafonio*. Milan: Suvini-Zerboni, 1958.

DA-237   Waterhouse, J. "Dallapiccola: Diatonicism and Dodecaphony," *Listener* 122 (1964): 641.

DA-238   "Werkeverzeichnis Luigi Dallapiccola," *Schweizerische Musikzeitung* 115, n. 4 (1975): 207-217.
           A complete catalogue of the works of Luigi Dallapiccola.

DA-239   Wildberger, J. "Dallapiccola's *Cinque Canti*," *Melos* 26 (Jan. 1959): 7-10.
           A discussion of the *Cinque Canti* composition of Luigi Dallapiccola.

DA-240   _____. "Les grandes heures de Luigi Dallapiccola pour l'histoire de la musique," *Musique en Jeu* n. 21 (Nov. 1975): 67-80.

DA-241   _____. "Dallapiccolas *Job*," *Melos* 21 (July-Aug. 1954): 208-210.

DA-242   _____. "Luigi Dallapiccolas musikgeshichtliche sternstunde," *Schweizerische Musikzeitung* 115, n. 4 (1975): 171-175.

DA-243   Wimbush, R. "Luigi Dallapiccola," *Grammophone* 45 (Nov. 1967): 254-255.

DA-244   Zanolini, B. *Luigi Dallapiccola -- La conquista di un linguaggio*. Padova: G. Zanibon, 1974.
           The author has given a chronological exposé of the creative output of Dallapiccola from 1928-1941. Vocal works are covered in Chapter 1, and instrumental works are discussed in Chapter 2. *Tre Laudi* and the *Canti di Prigionia* are critiqued in Chapter 3. Musical examples are plentiful and helpful. Reviews are found in *Nuova Rivista Musicale Italiana* 10, n. 2 (1976): 287-288, and *Schweizerische Musikzeitung* 117, n. 3 (1977): 172.

DA-245   Zimmerman, C. "Aachen," *Oper und Konzert* 23, n. 7 (1985): 2-3.
                    A concise discussion of the Dallapiccola opera *Il
             Prigioniero.*

DONATONI, FRANCO

DO-246   Brindle, Reginald S.   :The Lunatic Fringe: Computational
          Composition," *Musical Times* 97 (July 1956): 354-356.

DO-247   Castagnino, S. "Italy: Donatoni Premiere," *Opera* 36 (June 1985):
          675-677.
          The premiered work is Donatoni's *Atem*.

DO-248   Donatoni, Franco. *Antecedent X*. Milan: Adelphi 1980.
          A review in contained in *Rivista Musicale Italiana* 16,
          n. 2 (1982): 255-259.

DO-249   _____. "Para un diario 62/76," *Pauta* 2, n. 6 (1983): 91-93.
          The article is translated from the book *Autobiografia
          de la Musica Contemporanea* (compiled by Michele Mollia).

DO-250   Gava, E. "Milano," *Musica d'Oggi* 3 (Jan. 1960): 23-24.

DO-251   "Les mal entendus -- compositeurs des annees 70," *La Revue Musicale*
          n. 314-315: 47-52, n. d.

DO-252   Piamonte, G. "A Milano," *Nuova Rivista Musicale Italiana* 10, n. 2
          (1976): 338-339.

DO-253   Pinzanti, L. " A colloquio con Franco Donatoni," *Nuova Rivista
          Musicale Italiana* 4 (Mar.-Apr. 1970): 399-307.

DO-254   _____. "Da Siena," *Nuova Rivista Musicale Italiana* 10, n. 4
          (1976): 647-648.

EVANGELISTI, FRANCO

EV-255   Bachmann, C. H. "Theorie und Praxis improvisierter Musik; über ein musikalisches Phänomen der Gegenwart," *Neue Zeitschrift für Musik* 132 (Oct. 1971): 531+, *Musik und Bildung* 5 (May 1973): 232-242.
An article which discusses the theory and practice of improvised music. Evangelisti is mentioned in this regard, and his insight into these concepts is critiqued.

EV-256   Evangelisti, F. "Avantgard och musikalisk foerveckling," *Nutida Musik* 21 (1977-1978): 4-7.
Biographical information about the composer is given.

EV-257   _____. "Komponisten improvisieren al Kollehtiv," *Melos* 33 (Mar. 1966): 86-88.
This article gives a critiqué of aleatoric improvisation. Several composers (including the composer) participate in improvisational sessions held in Europe and California, and these events are also discussed.

EV-258   "Franco Evangelisti," *Nutida Musik* 14, n. 3 (1970-1971): 6, n. a.

EV-259   "Franco Evangelisti," *Santa Cecilia* 11 (1970-1971): 34-35, n. a.
Biographical information about the composer is provided.

EV-260   Tobeck, C. "Franco Evangelisti, *Proiezione sonore*," *Nutida Musik* 28, n. 3 (1984-1985): 12.
A consideration of the *Proiezione sonore* work of Franco Evangelisti.

ITALIAN DODECAPHONY

IT-261   Alsina, C. R. (and others). "Kann ein Komponist von Komponieren leben?" *Melos* 36 (Apr. 1969): 158-159, 163-164.
         28 composers discuss the following pertinent question for music activity in the twentieth-century: "Can a composer compose for a living?" Among others, Donatoni (p. 158-159) and Petrassi (p. 163-164) give comments.

IT-262   Barry, M. "New and Modern," *Music and Musicians* 26 (Jul. 1978): 50-51.

IT-263   Brindle, Reginald S. "The Origins of Italian Dodecaphony," *Musical Times* 97 (Feb. 1956): 75-76.

IT-264   Bortolotto, M. "Alla ricerca della nuovo musica," *Musica d'Oggi* 7, n. 4 (1964): 104-107.

IT-265   _____. *Faseseconda: study sulla nuova musica.* Turin, 1969, n. p.

IT-266   _____. "Italy -- New Music at Palermo," *Perspectives of New Music* 2, n. 2 (1964): 160-161.
         The works of composers Clementi, Evangelisti, Berio, Togni, Donatoni, and Bussotti are discussed.

IT-267   _____. "New Music in Italy," *Musical Quarterly* 51, n. 1 (1965): 61-77.
         Admiring yet discriminating comment on works by Nono, Berio, Castiglioni, Evangelisti, Clementi, Togni, Bussotti, Donatoni, and Vlad.

IT-268   _____. "Nowa muzyka we Wloszech (trans. H. Krzeczkowski)," *Ruch Muzyczny* 6, n. 10 (1962): 11-13.

The composers Castiglioni, Berio, Donatoni, Nono,
and Clementi are named in regard to discussion of their work.

IT-269   Collaer, P. *La musique moderne*. Bruxelles: Elsevier, 1963.

IT-270   Casella, A. "Neue italiensche Musik," *Melos* 25 (Jan. 1958): 10-12.

IT-271   DePaoli, Domenico. *La Crisis musicale Italiani*. Milan, 1939, n. p.

IT-272   Gatti, Guido. M. "Italy," *Musical Quarterly* 35 (Jan. 1949): 134-141,
          (Oct. 1949): 632-637.
                    Compositions of Dallapiccola and Petrassi are
          critiqued.

IT-273   _____. "Nuovi aspectti della situazione musicale in Italia," *La
          Rassegna Musicale* 7 (Gennaio-Febbraio 1934): 29-38.
                    The composers Dallapiccola and Petrassi are
          esteemed by the author to be in the forefront of progressive
          compositional activity in Italy; their musical progress is thus
          discussed.

IT-274   Germani, F. "A Glimpse of the Italian Scene," *Canon* 10 (Nov. 1956):
          109-112.

IT-275   Glickman, M. "New Sounds Amid Old," *Musical Courier* 163 (June
          1961): 15-16.
                    The musical activities of Petrassi, Nono, Maderna,
          Dallapiccola, and Vlad are discussed (among other modern
          non-serial Italian composers) in an article which attempts to
          describe the change in the aesthetic of Italian composition:
          from the traditional ideologies to the new "pointillist" school.

IT-276   Haglund, R. "Musikmosaik oever det rike nutida Italien," *Musikrevy*
          35, n. 4-5 (1980): 183+.
                    The composers Donatoni (p. 186+), Togni (p. 189),
          Maderna (p. 190), Vlad (p. 190), Clementi (p. 184),
          Castiglioni (p. 183), and Dallapiccola (p. 185) are discussed
          as to their prominence in the Italian avant-garde.

IT-277   Hambraeus, B. "Kring den unga italienska musiken," *Musikrevy* 20,
          n. 5-6 (1965): 232-236.

IT-278   Knockaert, Y. "Vokale werken van Luciano Berio en Luigi Nono," *Revue Belge de Musicologie* 31 (1977): 142-152.
Berio's *Sequenza III* and Luigi Nono's *Il Canto Sospeso* are analyzed after brief biographies on each composer are given. Included also are bibliographies, plenty of illustrations, and musical examples.

IT-279   La Pegna, D. "New Musical Works in Italy," *Musical Europe* 1 (Autumn 1950): 22-23.

IT-280   MacDonald, C. "Dallapiccola and Petrassi," *Tempo* n. 122 (Sept. 1977): 34-35.
The compositions discussed are *Three Questions with Two Answers* for orchestra (Dallapiccola) and *Orations Christi* for chorus, brass, violas, and violoncellos (Petrassi).

IT-281   Malipiero, G. F. "Contemporary Music in Italy," *Score and IMA Magazine* n. 15 (Mar. 1956): 7-9.

IT-282   Mann, R. W. "Italian Composers of Today," *London Musical Events* 8 (Sept. 1953): 22-23.

IT-283   Michalke, Georg. "Italiens Musikernachwuchs," *Musikblätter* 2 (1950): 28-30.
The works of Dallapiccola and Petrassi (and Ghedini) are discussed.

IT-284   Mila, M. *La musique en Italie durant et aprés la guerre L'age nouveau.* 1951, n. p.

IT-285   _____. "Venezia," *La Rassegna Musicale* 29, n. 3 (1959): 264-265.

IT-286   Nickson, N. "A 20th-Century Revival -- A Brief Introduction to Some Aspects of the Rise of Modern Italian Music," *Miscellanea Musicologica -- Adelaide Studies in Musicology* 2 (Mar. 1967): 15-19.

IT-287   Parmentola, K. "Problem: na suvremennata italianska muzika," *Nutida Musik* 18, n. 4 (1974-1975): 24-29.
A critique of the accessibility of Italian music as represented in the musical scores of Berio, Bussotti, Clementi, Donatoni, Evangelisti, and Petrassi.

IT-288 Pestalozza, L. "I composition milanesi del doppoguerra," *La Rassegna Musicale* 27 (Mar. 1957): 28-43.
Among other composers discussed are Berio, Castiglioni, and Maderna. The musical activity of each composer is critiqued, and biographies are provided as well.

IT-289 Pinzauti, L. "Da Siena," *Nuova Rivista Musicale Italiana* 9, n. 3 (1975): 423-470.
Petrassi's *Ode a Dallapiccola* and Donatoni's *Lumen* are discussed.

IT-290 Prieberg, Fred K. "Italiens electronische Musik," *Melos* 25 (June 1958): 194-198.

IT-291 _____. *Lexicon der neuen Musik.* 1958, n. p.
The Italians Berio, Dallapiccola, Maderna, Nono, Togni, and Vlad receive discussion and critique (among others).

IT-292 Steinecke, Wolfgang, edit. *Darmstädter Beiträge zur Neuen Musik.* Vol. 2. Mainz: Schott, 1959.
Articles on Berio and Nono are included in this important new music periodical.

IT-293 Stuckenschmidt, H. *La musical del XX secolo.* Milano: Saggiatore, 1969.

IT-294 Testa, S. E. "Atonalita and Dodecaphonia in Italy to 1935," *Dissertation Abstracts* 43 (May 1983): 3453A.
A captivating study of non-tonal Italian art music (written in the 20th-Century).

IT-295 Vinton, John. *Dictionary of 20th-Century Music.* London: Thames and Hudson, 1974, p. 354-358.
An excellent discussion of the musical activity of Italian dodecaphonic and avant-garde composers.

IT-296 Vlad, Roman. "Den italienska musik -- situation efter sista Kriget," *Musikrevy* 15, n. 3-4 (1960): 111-115.

IT-297 _____. *Modernita e tradizione nell a musica contemporanea.* Turin: 1955, n. p.

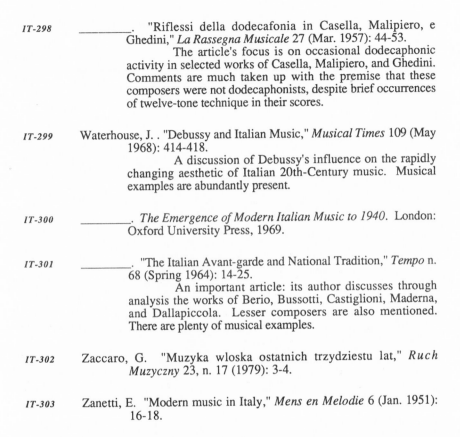

IT-298   _____. "Riflessi della dodecafonia in Casella, Malipiero, e Ghedini," *La Rassegna Musicale* 27 (Mar. 1957): 44-53.
The article's focus is on occasional dodecaphonic activity in selected works of Casella, Malipiero, and Ghedini. Comments are much taken up with the premise that these composers were not dodecaphonists, despite brief occurrences of twelve-tone technique in their scores.

IT-299   Waterhouse, J. . "Debussy and Italian Music," *Musical Times* 109 (May 1968): 414-418.
A discussion of Debussy's influence on the rapidly changing aesthetic of Italian 20th-Century music. Musical examples are abundantly present.

IT-300   _____. *The Emergence of Modern Italian Music to 1940.* London: Oxford University Press, 1969.

IT-301   _____. "The Italian Avant-garde and National Tradition," *Tempo* n. 68 (Spring 1964): 14-25.
An important article: its author discusses through analysis the works of Berio, Bussotti, Castiglioni, Maderna, and Dallapiccola. Lesser composers are also mentioned. There are plenty of musical examples.

IT-302   Zaccaro, G. "Muzyka wloska ostatnich trzydziestu lat," *Ruch Muzyczny* 23, n. 17 (1979): 3-4.

IT-303   Zanetti, E. "Modern music in Italy," *Mens en Melodie* 6 (Jan. 1951): 16-18.

MADERNA, BRUNO

MA-304   Baroni, M. and Dalmonte, Rossana, edit. *Bruno Maderna: Documenti*. Milan: Suvini Zerboni, 1985.

MA-305   Brindle, Reginald S. "Current Chronicle -- Italy," *Musical Quarterly* 45 (1959): 388-392.
A discussion of the *String Quartet* in two movements and *Serenada No. 2* for 11 instruments. Also included in the article is biographical information on the composer.

MA-306   "Bruno Maderna," *Music and Musicians* 22 (Oct. 1973): 7-8, n. a.
Maderna's *3rd Oboe Concerto* is discussed as well as activities in electronic composition and conducting.

MA-307   "Bruno Maderna," *Santa Cecilia* 9, n. 5 (1960): 7-8, n. a.
A biography of the composer is given along with a portrait.

MA-308   "Bruno Maderna," *Santa Cecilia* 11 (Apr. 1962): 42-43, n. a.
Biographical information on the composer is given; a list of principal compositions are provided as well.

MA-309   "Bruno Maderna," *Schweizerische Musikzeitung* 97 (June 1957): 233.
Included in this exposé of Maderna's musical career is a list of compositions.

MA-310   Fearn, R. "At the Doors of Kranichstein: Maderna's *Fantasia for 2 Pianos*," *Tempo* 163 (Dec. 1987): 14-20.
Analytic discourse on Maderna's *Fantasia for 2 Pianos*.

MA-311   _____. "Bruno Maderna: From the Cafe Pedrocchi to Darmstädt,"
                Tempo 155 (Dec. 1985): 8-14.
                A well-written article; it provides much needed
                retrospective discussion about Maderna as well as his music.
                Musical examples are present in this article also.

MA-312   Gallarati, P. "Da Torina," *Nuova Rivista Musicale Italiana* 9, n. 4
                (1975): 622-625.

MA-313   Grubertoni, A. "Le fonte poetiche dell' *Hyperion* di Bruno Maderna,"
                Nuova Rivista Musicale Italiana 15, n. 2 (1981): 197+.

MA-314   Jansen, K. "Bruno Maderna and Dutch Concert Life," *Keynotes* 11
                (Sept. 1980): 30-36.

MA-315   Koegler, H. "Cologne," *Opera* 13 (June, 1962): 402-403.

MA-316   Manzoni, G. "Bruno Maderna," *Young Composers -- Die Reihe* 4
                (Bryn Mawr, 1960 -- germ. ed. 1958): 115-120.
                A critique of the compositional procedure and
                ideology of Bruno Maderna. The article is quite informative; it
                reveals much that is essential to an understanding of
                Maderna's music.

MA-317   Mila, M. *Maderna, musicista Europea.* Turin: Einaudi, 1976.
                A review is contained in *Schweizerische
                Musikzeitung* 116, n. 5. (1976): 406.

MA-318   Mindszenthy, J. "Amsterdam," *Opera News* 32 (Sept. 23, 1967):
                24-25.

MA-319   Morgan, R. P. "The New Pluralism," *High Fidelity/Musical America*
                31 (Mar. 1981): 56-58+.

MA-320   Pinzauti, L. "A colloquio con Bruno Maderna," *Nuova Rivista
                Musicale Italiana* 6, n. 4 (1972): 545-552.

MA-321   _____. "La lezione di Maderna," *Nuova Rivista Musicale Italiana*
                14, n. 3 (1980): 393+.

MA-322   Porter, A. "Holland," *Musical Times* 108 (Aug. 1967): 732-733.

MA-323   Romano, J. "Bruno Maderna," *Buenos Aires Musical* 19, n. 315
         (1964): 5-6.

MA-324   Samana, L. "Maderna's Derde Hobo concert," *Mens en Melodie* 30
         (Feb. 1975): 42-45.

MA-325   Soria, D. J. "Artist Life," *High Fidelity/Musical America* 21 (June
         1971): MA 4-6.

MA-326   "Un inedito di Bruno Maderna," *Nuova Rivista Musicale Italiana* 12, n.
         4 (1978): 517-520.
                         An introduction by Luciano Berio begins this article.

MA-327   Weber, H. "Bologna: Omaggio a Bruno Maderna," *Schweizerische
         Musikzeitung* 123, n. 4 (1983): 239+.

MA-328   Werker, G. "Mokken om Maderna," *Mens en Melodie* 22 (Jan. 1967):
         18-21.

MA-329   Wilks, J. "Dartington Course in Electronic Music," *Score* 28 (Jan.
         1961): 71-72.

NONO, LUIGI

NO-330   Alcavez, J. A. "Conversacion con Luigi Nono," *Buenos Aires Musical* 21, n. 347 (1966): 5.

NO-331   "Az oszfalyhare; beszelgetes Luigi Nonoval," *Muzika* 13 (Aug. 1970): 28-29.

NO-332   Bachmann, C. "Witten/Ruhr: Spectrum des Komponierens," *Schweizerische Musikzeitung* 113, n. 4 (1973): 229-231.

NO-333   Baruch, G. W. "Der sanfte Revolutionaer; 'Atelier Luigi Nono' im Sueddeutschen Rundfunk Stuttgart," *Neue Zeitschrift für Musik* n. 10 (Oct 1984): 32-33.

NO-334   Bek, J. "K problemu neoavantgardy," *Hudebni Veda* 21, n. 3 (1984): 251-259.

NO-335   Borris, S. "Luigi Nono -- zur Problematik engagierter Musik," *Musik und Bildung* 4 (June 1972): 289-291.

NO-336   Bracanin, P. "The Abstract System as Compositional Matrix--An Examination of Some Applications by Nono, Boulez, and Stockhausen," *Studies in Music* 5 (1971): 90-114.

NO-337   Brindle, Reginald, S. "Italy," *Musical Times* 96 (Jan. 1955): 41.

NO-338   _____. "Italy," *Musical Quarterly* 53, n. 1 (1967): 95-100.
An exposé of one of several "political" works of Nono; analytical procedures reveal the effect of this music on the human psyche. Included also in this article is an excerpt from the composition.

NO-339   De Pablo, L. "La formalistica musical actual como centro evolutivo," *Rivista Musical Chilena* 15, n. 78 (1961): 49-63.

NO-340   Duemling, A. "'Ich habe viel lieber die Konfusion': Luigi Nonos Bekenntnis zu offenem Denken; ein Gespräch," *Neue Zeitschrift für Musik* n. 2 (Feb. 1987): 22-28.
An interview with the Luigi Nono on compositional matters; a portrait and music manuscript excerpt is also provided.

NO-341   Einemann, Marita. "Luigi Nono -- die unendliche Bereitschaft zum Suchen," *Neue Zeitschrift für Musik* n. 5 (May 1984): 16-19.
An informative discussion of Nono's compositional habits. A portrait is included along with a representative notation excerpt.

NO-342   Fabian, I. "Die Avantgarde der Sechzigeriahre hat einen bekommen: Luigi Nonos *Intolleranza* and der Hamburgischen Staatsoper," *Opern Welt* 26, n. 4 (1985): 19-20.

NO-343   Faltin, P. "Luigi Nono," *Slovenska Hudba* 12, n. 4 (1968): 171-174.

NO-344   "Firebrand of Venice," *Opera News* 29 (Feb. 13, 1965): 6, n. a.
Biographical information is given, along with a portrait of the composer.

NO-345   Flammer, E. H. "Form und Gehalt -- eine Analyse von Luigi Nonos *La Fabbrica Illuminata*," *Melos/Neue Zeitschrift für Musik* 3, n. 3 (1977): 401-411.
An extensive analysis of the Nono composition *La Fabbrica Illuminata*.

NO-346   _____. *Politisch engagierte Musik als kompositoriasches Problem, dargestellt am Beispiel von Luigi Nono und Hans Werner Henze.* Baden-Baden: V. Koerner, 1981.
A review is in *Neue Zeitschrift für Musik* n. 6-7 (Jun.-Jul. 1982): 85-86.

NO-347   Gallarati, P. "A Torino," *Nuova Rivista Musicale Italiana* 9, n. 4 (1975): 675-676.
Discussion of the Nono works *Como una ola defuerza y luz* and *Ein Gespenst geht um in der Welt.*

NO-348 _____. "Da Torino," *Nuova Rivista Musicale Italiana* 11, n. 1 (1977): 80-83.
Discussion of Nono's composition *A floresta e jovem e cheja de vida.*

NO-349 Garavaglia, R., interviewer. "Luigi Nono's 'neuer Weg'," *Schweizerische Musikzeitung* 121, n. 5 (1981): 309+.
The Nono compositions *Das atmende Klarsien* and *Il Prometeo* are discussed.

NO-350 Gentilucci, A. "La technica corale di Luigi Nono," *Rivista Italiana di Musicologia* 2, n. 1 (1967): 111-129.
An important critique of the choral compositions of Luigi Nono; abundant musical examples are provided.

NO-351 Gilbert, J. M. "Dialectic Music: An Analysis of Luigi Nono's *Intolleranza*," *Dissertation Abstracts* 40 (Apr. 1980): 5240A.
An analysis of Nono's opera *Intolleranza 1960* through exploration of stylistic traits and political message (dialectic music).

NO-352 Henius, C. "Erfahrungen mit Luigi Nonos *La Fabbrica Illuminata* -- Dokumente, Arbeitsnotizen und Berichte," *Melos/Neue Zeitschrift für Musik* 41, n. 2 (1975): 102-108.

NO-353 Hopkins, G. W. "Luigi Nono," *Music and Musicians* 14 (Apr. 1966): 32-35+.
A biography and portrait is given along with a critique of Nono's compositions. Musical examples are abundant.

NO-354 "'Ich will das Bewusstsein meiner Mitmenschen reraendern' -- Gespräch mit Luigi Nono," *Opern Welt* 6: 20-21, n. a., n. d.

NO-355 "*Il Canto Sospeso*," *Musica* 10 (Dec. 1956): 855, n. a.

NO-356 Joachim, H. "*Il Canto Sospeso*: das neue Chorwerk des italienischen Komponisten," *Neue Zeitschrift für Musik* 118 (Feb. 1957): 103.
A discussion of Nono's *Il Canto Sospeso.*

NO-357 Jungheinrich, H. K. "Das grosse Abflauen nach den fuenfiziger Jahren; Darmstädter Ferienkurse für neue Musik," *HIFI/Stereophonie* 19 (Aug. 1980): 906-909.

NO-358 _____. "Het nieuwe luisteren naar Luigi Nono's *Prometheus*," *Mens en Melodie* 40 (Mar. 1985): 147-149.

NO-359 Klueppelholz, W. "Zur Soziologie der Neuen Musik," *International Review of the Aesthetics and Sociology of Music* 10, n. 1 (1979): 73-87.
A discussion of the sociological implication of New Music. Included are summaries of this article in English and Croatian. Avant-garde composers mentioned in the article include Nono, Stockhausen, and Ligeti.

NO-360 Koch, G. R. "Leiden und Schoenheit der Revolution," *Das Orchester* 26 (Nov. 1978): 842-846.

NO-361 Kolleritsche, O. "Musik zwischen Engagement und Kunst," *Musik und Bildung* 8: 549-551, n. d.

NO-362 Kramer, Jonathan. "The Fibonacci Series in Twentieth-Century Music," *Journal of Music Theory* 17, n. 1 (1973): 110-148.
Among other composers discussed is Nono; his composition *Il Canto Sospeso* is critiqued in the demonstration of the fibonacci phenomenon. An informative and important article.

NO-363 Lachenmann, H. "Luigi Nono," *Schweizerische Musikzeitung* 119, n. 5 (1979): 324-325.

NO-364 _____. "Luigi Nono oder Ruckblick auf die serielle Musik," *Melos* 38 (1971): 225-230.
Analysis of several Nono compositions are presented in the article; serial procedure and methodology in the works are mentioned as well. Musical examples are abundant.

NO-365 Lindlar, H. "Hiobsklage, Liebesballet 12-ton Sinfonik," *Musica* 9 (Aug. 1955): 388-389.

NO-366 Lueck, H. "Luigi Nono -- Musik für den Klassenkampft," *Neue Musikzeitung* 19, n. 2 (1970): 3.

NO-367 "Luigi Nono," *Santa Cecilia* 11 (Apr. 1962): 35-36, n. a.
Biographical information and a list of principal works is given.

NO-368 "Luigi Nono berichtet aus Italian -- Auseinandersetzungen jetzt auch in der Musik," *Schweizerische Musikzeitung* 119, n. 5 (1979): 284+.

NO-369 "Luigi Nono '. . . sofferte onde serene . . .'," *Schweizerische Musikzeitung* 117, n. 3 (1977): 160-161.

NO-370 Markowski, L. "Kammermusik: Pollini, Nono, und Andere," *Musik und Gesellschaft* 27 (Dec. 1977): 713-716.

NO-371 Martine, Cadieu. "Duo avec Luigi Nono," *Nouvelles Literaires* (April. 13, 1961): 1.

NO-372 Marothy, J. "Socialismus -- aktualni hudebni otazka," *Hudebni Veda* 15, n. 2 (1978): 100-102.

NO-373 Mayer, H. "De componist Luigi Nono," *Mens en Melodie* 25 (June 1970): 167-170.

NO-374 _____. "Luigi Nono, een hedendaags Italiaans componist," *Mens en Melodie* 17 (Jan. 1962): 9-12.

NO-375 Metger, H. K., and Riehn, R. edit. *Luigi Nono*. Munich: Text und Kritik, 1981.
A review in contained in *Neue Zeitschrift für Musik* 2 (Feb. 1982): 67.

NO-376 Mila, M. "La linea Nono," *La Rassegna Musicale* 30, n. 4 (1960): 297-311.
The composition *Il Canto Sospeso* is discussed after a lengthy introduction.

NO-377 Mueller, G. "Geschichte und Aesthetik zu den Opern konzeptionen Hanns Eislers, Luigi Nonos und Giacomo Manzonis," *Musik und Gesellschaft* 36 (Jun. 1986): 296-302.

NO-378 Neef, S. "Kammermusik *Guai ai gelidi mostri* von Luigi Nono," Musik und Gesellschaft 35 (Oct. 1985): 566-567.

A premier of the Nono composition *Guai ai gelidi mostri* is critiqued.

NO-379   Nono, Luigi. "Appunti per un teatro musicale attuale," *La Rassegna Musicale* 31, n. 4 (1961): 418-424.
          This article has been translated and published in *Pauta* 2, n. 8 (1983): 49-56.

NO-380   _____. "Die Entwicklung der Reihetechnik," *Darmstädter Beiträge zur Neuen Musik* 1: (1958) 57-81.

NO-381   _____. "Gitterstabe an Himmel der Freihert," *Melos* 27 (Mar. 1960): 67-75.
          A transcription of a lecture given at Darmstädt on trends in music.

NO-382   _____. "*Intolleranza 1960* poznamky k hudobnemu divadlu sucasnosti," *Slovenska Hudba* 8, n. 7 (1964): 194-200.

NO-383   _____. "The Historical Reality of Music Today," *Score* 27 (June 1960): 41-45.

NO-384   _____. *Texte; Studien zu seiner Musik.* Edit. by Jurg Stenzl. Zurich: Atlantis, 1975.
          Reviews are in several periodicals:
          Schweizerische Musikzeitung 115, n. 6 (1975): 331.
          Musica 30, n. 5 (1976): 433.
          HIFI/Stereophonie 16 (Mar. 1977): 290+.
          Neue Musikzeitung 25, n. 6 (1976): 17.
          Nuova Rivista Musicale Italiana 10, n. 4 (1976): 681-683.
          Muzsika 20 (June 1977): 46-47.
          Musikerziehung 31 (Feb. 1978): 191.
          Ruch Muzyczny 23, n. 17 (1979): 12.
          Studies in Music 19, n. 1-4 (1977): 454-456.

NO-385   Oehlschlaegal, R. "Non consumiamo Luigi Nono--Kompositorische Entpolitisierung politischer Text," *Musica* 25, n. 6 (1977): 593-594.

NO-386   Pestalozza, L. "Luigi Nono," *Rivista Musical Chilena* 17, n. 85 (1963): 79-100.

NO-387 _____. "Osvobozeni a smrt v hudbe Luigi Nono," *Hudebni Rozhledy* 23, n. 5 (1970): 202.

NO-388 Pinzauti, L. "A colloquio con Luigi Nono," *Nuova Rivista Musicale Italiana* 4 (Jan.-Feb. 1970): 69-81.

NO-389 _____. "Rozhovors Luigi Nonom," *Hudbni Rozhledy* 23, n. 6 (1970): 267-271.

NO-390 _____. "Lo Sherlock Holmes di Napoli," *Nuova Rivista Musicale Italiana* 4 (Mar.-Apr. 1970): 320-321.

NO-391 Pone, G. "Webern and Luigi Nono: The Genesis of a New Compositional Morphology and Syntax," *Perspectives of New Music* 10, n. 2 (1972): 111-119.
The article discusses the close relationship between pure musical utterance and speech. The compositions of Nono are addressed in this regard; they are also compared with the compositional ideology of Webern.

NO-392 Pulido, E. "En la orbita de Luigi Nono," *Heterofonia* 4: 5-8, n. d.

NO-393 Riis-Vestergaard, H. "Luigi Nono: *Il Canto Sospeso*," *Dansk Musiktidsskrift* 40, n. 1 (1965): 17-18.

NO-394 Rosing-Schow, A. "Luigi Nono: Musikmellem realitet og utopi," *Dansk Musiktidsskrift* 59, n. 1 (1984-1985): 25-28.

NO-395 Rostand, C. "Pariser Kirche und Theatre im Zeichen neuer Musik," *Melos* 22 (June 1955): 182-184.

NO-396 Skrzynska, A. "Jesienne refleksje," *Ruch Muzyczny* 19, n. 24 (1975): 5-7.

NO-397 Sprangemacher, F. "Hiroshima in der Musik: Bemerkungen zu einigen Kompositionen mit dem Thema der nuklearen Bedrohung," *Schweizerische Musikzeitung* 120, n. 2 (1980): 78-88.

NO-398 _____. "Komposition als Herausforderung: Luigi Nono wird 60," *Musik und Bildung* 16 (Jan 1984): 30-36.
A discography, biography, and portrait in included in this critique of Luigi Nono's artistic legacy.

NO-399   _____. *Luigi Nono: die electronische Musik; historicher Kontext -- Entwichlung-Kompositions technik.* Regensburg: G. Bosse, 1983.

A book containing detailed discourse on Nono's compositional output and procedure. Reviews are found in the following journals:

Musica 38, n. 1 (1984): 72.
Neue Zeitschrift für Musik n. 7-8 (Jul.-Aug. 1983) : 68.
Oesterreichische Musikzeitschrift 39 (Jan. 1984): 53.
Das Orchester 32 (May 1984): 460.

NO-400   _____. "Resonanzen des Fragens und Suchens: ein neues Werk von Luigi Nono," *Neue Zeitschrift für Musik* n. 5 (1987): 43-44.

A critique of a new work, *Risonanze errante*, by Nono is offered.

NO-401   Stein, L. "New Music on Monday," *Perspectives of New Music* 2 (Fall-Winter 1963): 147-148.

The Nono composition *Ha venido* is mentioned. A musical example is given also.

NO-402   Stenzl, Jurg. "Luigi Nono und Cesare Parese," *Darmstädter Beiträge zur Neuen Musik* 14: (1974) 93-119.

NO-403   _____. "Nonos *Incontri*," *Melos* 39, n. 3 (1972): 150-153.

An analysis of Nono' s *Incontri*; a graph which projects how several parameters of music work in the composition is provided as well.

NO-404   Stockhausen, Karlheinz. "Music and Speech," *Die Reihe* 6 (1964): 40-64.

Another article which compares the close relationship between pure musical utterance and human speech. Thus, a critique of *Il Canto Sospeso* is provided. Plenty of musical examples are present in this informative article. The article can be found also in *Darmstädter Beiträge zur Neuen Musik* 1: (1958) 57-81.

NO-405   Stuerzbecherm, V. "Das grosse Fragezeichen hinter einer gesellschaftspolitischen Function der Musik," *Melos* 39, n. 3 (1972): 142.

A discussion of how "political music" works. Nono's contribution to this kind of music aesthetic is mentioned.

NO-406 Stuckenschmidt, H. H. "Aspecte des Todes -- musiklisch gedeutet," *Musica* 29, n. 6 (1975): 495-496.

NO-407 Unger, U. "Luigi Nono," *Die Reihe* 4 (Bryn Mawr, 1960), germ. ed. 1958): 5-13.
An important article; it provides a discussion of the compositional ideology and work of Luigi Nono.

NO-408 Varnai, P. *Beszelgetesek Luigi Nonoval*. Budapest: Zenemukiado, 1978.
A review is presented in the periodical *Muzsika* 21 (Dec. 1978): 38-39.

NO-409 Vila, C., and Bodenhoefer, A. "Entrevista a Luigi Nono," *Rivista Musical Chilena* 25, n. 115-116 (1971): 3-9.

NO-410 "Visita de Luigi Nono," *Rivista Musical Chilena* 21, n. 102 (1967): 139-140.

NO-411 Vogt, H. "*Al Gran Sole* carico d'autocitazione -- oder: Zwischen Patchwork und Pasticco. Zur dramaturgisch-musikalischen Gestaltung der 2. szenischen Aktion *Al Gran Sole Carico d'amore* von Luigi Nono," *Neuland Ansaetze zur Musik der Gegenwart* 5 (1984-1985): 125-139.

NO-412 Von Lewinski, W. E. "Linke Toene -- schoene Toene: progressive Komponisten suchenihr Publikum," *Das Orchester* 20 (Sept. 1972): 441-442.

NO-413 _____. "Where Do We Go From Here: A European View," *Musical Quarterly* 55, n. 2 (1969): 195-196.
A discussion of the future direction of the European avant-garde. Composers mentioned include Nono, Stockhausen, and Boulez.

NO-414 Worbs, H. C. "Wegezum Hoever: Nono in Hamburg," *Musica* 39, n. 3 (1985): 286-287.

PETRASSI, GOFFREDO

PE-415   Albrecht, N. "Kammermusik im Gespräch: Goffredo Petrassi," *Musik und Gesellschaft* 34 (Aug. 1984): 445.

PE-416   Annabaldi, C., edit. "Alfredo Casella a Goffredo Petrassi--ventitre lettere inedite," *Nuova Rivista Musicale Italiana* 6, n. 4 (1972).

PE-417   _____, and Monna, M. *Bibliographia e catalogo delle opera di Goffredo Petrassi.* Milan: Suvini Zerboni, 1980.
          The book is reviewed in *Music and Letters* 66, n. 4 (1985): 383-385.

PE-418   Bellingardi, L. "Da Perugia," *Rivista Musicale Italiana* 16, n. 4 (1982): 629-633.
          A discussion of the premier of the Petrassi composition *Laudes Creaturum.*

PE-419   Bonelli, A. E. "Serial Techniques in the Music of Goffredo Petrassi: A Study of His Compositions from 1950-1959," *Dissertation Abstracts* 31 (Mar. 1971): 4813A.
          The year 1950 marks the beginning of dodecaphonic activity in Petrassi's music; works composed in this style are discussed in detail. Most informative are the conclusions drawn from these discussions (style traits of the composer).

PE-420   Bortolotto, M. "Petrassis Stil 1960," *Melos* 33 (Feb. 1966): 48-50.
          An analysis of the *Trio* for Violin, Viola, and Violoncello. Thematic fragments are given to help illustrate salient points.

PE-421   _____. "Zwei neue Werke von Goffredo Petrassi," *Melos* 30 (Apr. 1963): 114-117.

Two works, the *Serenade* and *String Quartet*, are analyzed. Thematic fragments and music examples are present.

PE-422   Briggs, J. "Composer with Style," *New York Times* 105, sect. 2 (Dec. 18, 1955): 9.
A crucial newspaper article; it contains quotes from Petrassi which address such subjects as his techniques of orchestration and dodecaphony. The composer provides also his perspective on the current musical trends.

PE-423   Costarelli, N. "La Toccata di Goffredo Petrassi e la Musica pura," *Musica d'Oggi* 19 (1973): 48-50.

PE-424   D'Amico, F. "La musica e l'impegno," *Nuova Rivista Musicale Italiana* 14, n. 3 (1980): 325-326.
A discussion of the Petrassi work *Beatitudines.*

PE-425   _____. "Petrassi e il suo Salmo," *La Rassegna Musicale* 11: 215-223, n. d.

PE-426   Gaburo, Kenneth. "Goffredo Petrassi: The Man and His Music," *Musical Courier* 154 (Sept. 1956): 6, 30.
A cordial introduction precedes Petrassi's biography; a critique of Petrassi's compositional output as well as stylistic traits follow.

PE-427   _____. "Lenox, Mass.," *Musical Quarterly* 42 (Oct. 1956): 530-533.
A brief analysis of the *Concerto No. 5* for orchestra is provided, with special emphasis on dodecaphonic procedures. Musical examples are abundant.

PE-428   Gatti, Guido, M. "Modern Italian Composers I: Goffredo Petrassi," *Monthly Musical Record* 67 (1937): 1-3.

PE-429   Gavazzeni, G. "Musiche di Petrassi," *Quadrente* (June 1936), Rome, n. ppg.

PE-430   Goddard, S. "A Bridge Restored," *Listener* 61 (Mar. 12, 1959): 486.

PE-431   "Goffredo Petrassi," *Santa Cecilia* 10, n. 5 (1961): 76, n. a.

                    Biographical information along with a portrait of the
          composer given.

PE-432   "Goffredo Petrassi," *Santa Cecilia* 11 (Apr. 1962): 32, n. a.
          Biographical information along with a list of
          compositions is given.

PE-433   "Goffredo Petrassi 75," *Musikhandel* 30, n. 6 (1979): 335, n. a.
          Biographical information is provided.

PE-434   Gruen, A. "Gitarren musik um 1960," *Gitarre & Laute* 8, n. 1 (1986):
          59-63.
          The Petrassi work *Suoni notturni* work is discussed.

PE-435   Haglund, R. "Petrassi i tiden," *Musikrevy* 35, n. 4-5 (1980): 194+.

PE-436   Lombardi, L. *Conversazioni con Petrassi.* Milan: Suvini Zerboni,
          1980.
          Interesting dialogue from the composer Petrassi
          about music. The book is reviewed in *Music and Letters* 66,
          n. 4 (1985): 383-385.

PE-437   _____. "Spannung vertritt die Form," *Neue Zeitschrift für Musik* n.
          3 (Mar. 1986): 21-25.
          An interview with Petrassi; discussed compositions
          are the *Concertos for Orchestra.*

PE-438   Maggini, L. "Goffredo Petrassi da *Estre* a *Ottavo Concerto,*" *Nuova
          Rivista Musicale Italiana* 9, n. 1 (1975): 64-96.

PE-439   Mila, M. "Italian löst sich von 19. Jahrundert," *Melos* 25 (Jun. 1958):
          185-189.

PE-440   Nowicki, A. "Muzyka policentryczna i kompozycje obdayzone moca
          retroaktywna," *Ruch Muzyczny* 29, n. 18 (1985): 18-19.
          The *Serenata* work of Petrassi is discussed.

PE-441   Pestalozza, L. "Il sentimento dell'assoluto in Goffredo Petrassi," *La
          Rassegna Musicale* 24 (Oct.-Dec. 1954): 318-327.
          An informative discussion of the early compositions
          as well as the works composed in the dodecaphonic style.

PE-442 "Petrassi," *London Musical Events* 27 (Oct. 1972): 24-25+, n. a.

PE-443 Ropioni, E. "Goffredo Petrassi," *Rivista Musical Chilena* 17, n. 85 (1963): 73-78.

PE-444 Stone, O. "Goffredo Petrassi's *Concerto for Pianoforte and Orchestra*: A Study of Twentieth-Century Neo-Classic Style," *Music Review* 39, n. 3-4 (1978): 240-257.
A wealth of musical examples accompany a wonderfully informative analysis of the Petrassi *Concerto*.

PE-445 _____. "Goffredo Petrassi's *Eight Inventions for Pianoforte*: A Study of Twentieth-Century Contrapuntal Style," *Music Review* 33, n. 3 (1972): 210-217.
A study of 20th-Century contrapuntal style through an analysis of the Petrassi *Inventions*. Included is a list of published works, illustrations, and plenty of musical examples.

PE-446 _____. "Petrassi's *Sonata da Camera for Harpsichord and Ten Instruments*: A Study of Twentieth-Century Linear Style," *Music Review* 37, n. 4 (1976): 283-294.
The *Sonata da Camera* of Petrassi is analyzed, and linear techniques are discussed. Musical examples are plentiful.

PE-447 _____. "Goffredo Petrassi's *Toccata for Pianoforte*: A Study of Twentieth-Century Toccata Style," *Music Review* 37, n. 1 (1976): 45-51.
An outright analysis of the *Toccata* (1933) and the *Eight Variations* (1944). Many musical examples are present.

PE-448 Szollozy, A., and Jeney, Z. "Petrassit koszontjuk," *Muzsika* 27 (July 1984): 3-9.

PE-449 Tapia, Godoy I. "Los tres-estilos de Goffredo Petrassi," *Rivista Musical Chilena* 16, n. 80 (1962): 45-52.

PE-450 Vlad, Roman. "Goffredo Petrassis Orchesterkonzert," *Melos* 26 (June 1959): 174-178.

PE-451 Waterhouse, J. C. "Petrassi 60," *Music and Musicians* 12 (July 1964): 12+.

54

*A SELECTED ANNOTATED BIBLIOGRAPHY
ON ITALIAN SERIAL COMPOSERS*

Biographical information is given, as well as a portrait of the composer.

PE-452 _____. A Review of Goffredo Petrassi Study Scores: *Poema, Sestina d'autunno 'Veni, creator Igor',* and *Laudes Creaturarum," Music and Letters* 66, n. 2 (1985): 193-195.
An analytically informative review of published Petrassi compositions (music publisher: Milan: Suvini Zerboni, 1982-1983).

PE-453 Weaver, W. "Florence," *Opera* 23 (1972): 108-113.
A discussion of the Petrassi work *Morte dell'aria* is here, as well as musical examples.

PE-454 Weissman, John S. *Goffredo Petrassi.* Milan: Suvini-Zerboni, 1960, 2nd ed. London: Boosey and Hawkes, 1980.
An interesting critique of the artistic legacy of Petrassi, with plenty of musical examples and a portrait of this composer. Twelve-tone analysis and discussion of Petrassi's music are focal points of discourse in the book. Reviews can be located in *Music and Letters* 39 (July 1958): 310-311, and *Musical Times* 122 (Oct. 1981): 674-675.

PE-455 _____. "Goffredo Petrassi, geb. 16. 7. 1904," *Melos* 31 (Jul.-Aug. 1964): 227-230.
The artistic legacy of Petrassi is discussed chronologically. Style traits and compositional ideology are mentioned also.

PE-456 _____. "Goffredo Petrassi and his Music," *Music Review* 22, n. 3 (1961): 198-211.
A substantial article covering the artistic legacy of Petrassi. Musical examples abound, and a list of works and bibliography are presented also.

PE-457 _____. "Petrassi in England," *London Musical Events* 14 (Feb. 1959): 17-18.

PE-458 _____. "Le prime compositional corali di Petrassi," *Musica d'Oggi* 2 (Oct. 1959): 342-346.

PE-459 _____. "Petrassi's *Tre per Setti* and *Estri,*" *Musical Quarterly* 61, n. 4 (1975): 588-594.

A well-conceived analysis of both compositions, with musical examples abundant.

PE-460   _____. "Le untime opera di Goffredo Petrassi," *La Rassegna Musicale* 22 (Apr. 1952): 113-122.
An important exposé of Petrassi's non-serial works. Among works cited are *Il Cordavano*, *Coro di Morti*, and *Sonata di Camera*.

TOGNI, CAMILLO

TO-461   Brindle, Reginald S.   "The Lunatic Fringe: Computational Composition," *Musical Times* 97 (July 1956): 355-356.
The op. 36 Togni composition *Ricercare* is discussed.

TO-462   "Camillo Togni," *La Rassegna Musicale* 20 (Apr. 1950): 134, n. a.
Included in the article is a complete list of compositions.

TO-463   "Camillo Togni," *Santa Cecilia* 11 (Apr. 1962): 31, n. a.
Biographical information is given as well as a list of principal compositions.

TO-464   Castagnino, S. "Milan," *Opera* 30 (Jan. 1979): 69-70.

TO-465   Cernaz, B. "Venice: teatro la Fenice," *Opera Canada* 19, n. 2 (1978): 33-34.
The article provides a biography of the life and musical activity of Camillo Togni.

TO-466   *"Fantasia Concertante* per flauto e orchestra d'arche," *La Rassegna Musicale* 29 (June 1959): 172-173, n. a.
The Togni composition *Fantasia Concertante* is discussed as to external form, compositional style, and rhythm.

TO-467   Rinaldi, M. "La grave crisi dell'Opera di Roma," *Rassegna Musicale Curci* 35, n. 1 (1982): 48-50.

TO-468   Piamonte, G. "Da Milano," *Nuova Rivista Musicale Italiana* 12, n. 4 (1978): 597-598.

VLAD, ROMAN

VL-469   Bonafini, V. "Da Mantova," *Nuova Rivista Musicale Italiana* 9, n. 3 (1975): 426-428.

VL-470   "Cork," *Musical Times* 107 (July 1966): 617-618, n. a.
The Vlad composition *Lettura di Michelangelo* is discussed.

VL-471   Gould, S. "Florentine vicissitudes," *Opera* 26 (Nov. 1975): 1025-1030.

VL-472   Graziosi, G. "Musicisti del nostro tempo -- Roman Vlad," *La Rassegna Musicale* 23 (Jan. 1953): 6-18.
A timely exposé of the compositional techniques, procedures, and ideology of Roman Vlad. Musical examples are given.

VL-473   Keller, Hans. "Film Music and Beyond," *Music Review* 12 (May 1951): 147-149.
An analysis of motion picture music composed by Roman Vlad.

VL-474   Pestelli, G. "Da Torino," *Nuova Rivista Musicale Italiana* 5 (Jul.-Aug. 1971): 681-683.
The Vlad composition *Il Gabbiano* is discussed.

VL-475   "Roman Vlad," *La Rassegna Musicale* 20 (Jan. 1950): 41-43. n. a.
Included within this article is a list of Vlad's compositions

VL-476   Stevenson, R. "An Introduction to the Music of Roman Vlad," *Music Review* 22, n. 2 (1961): 123-135.

      A biography of the composer begins this informative and equally important article. Vlad's compositional output is discussed subsequently (works from 1948 to 1955).

VL-477   Vlad, Roman. "I libre," *Nuova Rivista Musicale Italiana* 4 (May-June 1970): 570-574.

VL-478   _____. "Rilettura della *Sagra*," *Rivista Musicale Italiana* 17, n. 3-4 (1983): 426+.

II. AUTHOR/EDITOR INDEX

In the **Composer/Subject Index**, there are several entries which are listed without a given author (n. a.). In the **Author/Editor Index**, the entries can be located under the name of the referenced composer.

III. PERIODICAL/JOURNAL INDEX

American Society of University
    Composers DA-127

Broadcast Music, Inc. BE-20
Buenos Aires Musical MA-323, NO-330

Cahiers de la Musique DA-189, DA-226
Canadian Composer BE-18, BE-75
Canadian Music Book BE-3
Canadian University Music Review
    BE-1
Canon IT-274
Centerpoint BE-71, DA-125
Chesterian DA-159, DA-233
Chronache Musicale DA-199
Composer (U. S.) BE-33
Counterpoint DA-202

Dansk Musiktidsskrift BE-55, CA-112,
    NO-393, NO-394
Darmstädter Beiträge zur Neuen Musik
    BE-10, BE-46, IT-292, NO-380,
    NO-402, NO-404
Das Orchester DA-196, NO-360,
    NO-399, NO-412
Die Reihe BE-70, MA-316, NO-404,
    NO-407
Dissertation Abstracts BE-13, BE-38,
    BE-47, BE-51, BE-52, BE-53, BE-60,
    BE-69, BE-80, DA-140, DA-154,
    DA-173, DA-190, DA-191, DA-200,
    DA-217, IT-294, NO-351, PE-419

Electronic Music Review BE-64

Gitarre & Laute PE-434
Grammophone DA-243
Heterofonia NO-392
High Fidelity/Musical America BE-25,
    BE-36, BE-78, MA-319, MA-325
HIFI/Stereophonie BE-42, NO-357,
    NO-384
Horizon DA-232
Hudebni Rozhledy NO-387, NO-389
Hudebni Veda NO-334, NO-372

I casi della Musica DA-151
Il Trentino DA-213
Incontri Musicali BE-10
Interface/Journal of New Music
    Research BE-40, DA-157
International Review of the Aesthetics
    and Sociology of Music NO-359
Journal of Music Theory BE-21,
    DA-192, NO-362

Keynotes MA-314

L'Arche DA-187
L'Italia DA-212
La Radio DA-155
La Rassegna Musicale CA-117,
    DA-124, DA-153, DA-188, DA-198,
    DA-228, IT-273 IT-285, IT-288,
    IT-298, NO-376, NO-379, PE-425,
    PE-441, PE-460, TO-462, TO-466,
    VL-472, VL-475
La Revue Musicale BE-29, BE-41,
    BE-79, BE-84, BU-91, BU-92, BU-96
    DA-158 DO-251

Opern Welt BU-97, BU-101, BU-102,
    NO-342, NO-354
Organist Review BE-81

Pauta DO-249, NO-379
Perspectives of New Music BE-37,
    BE-83, BE-88, CA-113, DA-156,
    DA-163, DA-164, DA-203, DA-209,
    DA-210, IT-266, NO-391, NO-401

Quadrente PE-429
Quaderni della Rassegna Musicale
    DA-122, DA-123, DA-136, DA-147,
    DA-149, DA-167, DA-215, DA-219,
    DA-222, DA-229

Rassegna Musicale Curci BU-99,
    TO-467
Revue Belge de Musicologie BE-10,
    IT-278
Revue d' Esthetique BE-12
Rivista Italiana di Musicologia DA-138,
    NO-350
Rivista Musical Chilena DA-194,
    NO-339, NO-386, NO-409, NO-410,
    PE-443, PE-449
Rivista Musicale Italiana CA-115,
    DA-206, DA-223, DO-248, PE-418,
    VL-478
Royal College of Music DA-142
Ruch Muzyczny BE-17, IT-268, IT-302,
    NO-384, NO-396, PE-440

Santa Cecilia BE-50, CA-116, EV-259,
    MA-307, MA-308, NO-367, PE-431,
    PE-432, TO-463
Schweizerische Musikzeitung BE-11,
    BU-96, CL-119, DA-128, DA-161,
    DA-178, DA-182, DA-203, DA-207,
    DA-214, DA-238, DA-242, DA-244,
    MA-309, MA-317, MA-327, NO-332,
    NO-349, NO-363, NO-368, NO-369,
    NO-384, NO-397
*Score and IMA Magazine (known also
    as Score [1958-   ])* DA-141,
    DA-234, IT-281, MA-329, NO-383
Slovenska Hudba NO-343, NO-382
Societa DA-150
Sovetskaya Muzyka DA-176, DA-177,
    DA-180

Studies in Music DA-166, NO-336,
    NO-384

Tempo BE-58, DA-146, DA-195,
    DA-223, DA-235, IT-280, IT-301,
    MA-310, MA-311
Tibia BE-35
Tonfallet BE-61

Zeitschrift für Musik BE-4

IV. BOOK PUBLISHER INDEX

Baden-Baden: V. Koerner *NO-346*
Bruxelles: Elsevier *IT-269*
Budapest: Zenemukiado *DA-231,*
NO-408

Cambridge: Royal Musical
Association *BE-58*
Cologne: Gitarre & Laute *DA-179*

Florence, 1985, n. p. *DA-180*
Frankfurt: Suhrkamp *DA-227*

London: Boosey and Hawkes *PE-454*
London: Marian Boyars *BE-8*
London: Oxford University Press
IT-300
London: Thames and Hudson *IT-295*

Mainz: Schott *IT-292*
Milan: Adelphi *DO-248*
Milan: Arcadia *BE-21*
Milan: Ricordi *CA-115, DA-169*
Milan, 1939, n. p. *IT-271*
Milan: Saggiatore *DA-146, IT-293*
Milan: Suvini Zerboni *DA-144,*
DA-170, DA-207, DA-224, DA-233,
DA-236, MA-304, PE-417, PE-436,
PE-452, PE-454
Munich: Flade & Partner *BU-100*
Munich: Nymphenburger *BE-86*
Munich: Text und Kritik *NO-375*

Padova: G. Zanibon *DA-244*

Palermo: Novecento *BU-90*
Paris: Lattes *BE-22*
Paris: Seghers *DA-172*

Regensburg: G. Bosse *BE-28,*
NO-399

Toronto: University of Toronto Press
BE-6

Turin: Einaudi *MA-317*
Turin, 1969, n. p. *IT-265*
Turin, 1955, n. p. *IT-297*

Vienna: Universal *BE-2*

Zurich: Atlantis *NO-384*

No City or Publisher Given

1951, n. p. *IT-284*
1958, n. p. *IT-291*

Thesis/Dissertation (no located abstracts)

Ph.D. dissertation, University
College of North Wales *DA-137*
Unpublished Master's Thesis,
University of California: Berkeley
DA-126